# THE DEVILS
# AND CANON BARHAM

# BOOKS BY EDMUND WILSON

AXEL'S CASTLE

THE TRIPLE THINKERS

TO THE FINLAND STATION

THE WOUND AND THE BOW

THE SHOCK OF RECOGNITION

MEMOIRS OF HECATE COUNTY

CLASSICS AND COMMERCIALS

THE SHORES OF LIGHT

FIVE PLAYS

RED, BLACK, BLOND AND OLIVE

A PIECE OF MY MIND

THE AMERICAN EARTHQUAKE

APOLOGIES TO THE IROQUOIS

WILSON'S NIGHT THOUGHTS

PATRIOTIC GORE

THE COLD WAR AND THE INCOME TAX

O CANADA

THE BIT BETWEEN MY TEETH

EUROPE WITHOUT BAEDEKER

GALAHAD and I THOUGHT OF DAISY

A PRELUDE

THE DUKE OF PALERMO and OTHER PLAYS

THE DEAD SEA SCROLLS: 1947–1969

UPSTATE

A WINDOW ON RUSSIA

THE DEVILS AND CANON BARHAM

EDMUND WILSON

# The Devils
# and Canon Barham

*Ten Essays on Poets,*
*Novelists and Monsters*

Foreword by Leon Edel

FARRAR, STRAUS AND GIROUX
NEW YORK

The first six essays in this book appeared originally in *The New Yorker;* "*The Waste Land* in Déshabillé," "The Fruits of the MLA," and "The Monsters of Bomarzo" appeared in *The New York Review of Books;* " 'Baldini': A Memoir and a Collaboration with Edwin O'Connor" appeared in the *Atlantic Monthly.*

# CONTENTS

# FOREWORD
## by Leon Edel

*The Devils and Canon Barham* was Edmund Wilson's last "literary chronicle" in the long series that reminds us of Sainte-Beuve's *Causeries* but is so different: a gathering-in of his final essays, ten of them, written during the last four or five years of his life. Had he lived to read its galleys, he might have added a preface; he would most certainly have edited himself strenuously, and grafted in new material, in that unifying process by which his packed pieces became literary roadposts of the twentieth century. But the infirmities of his aging imposed restraints on his unyielding spirit; and he ironically referred to himself, in one of his serio-comic verses (for he was among other things a master of light verse) as "a monster of sloth"—

In the daytime I often fold up like a moth.
I lounge here so flat I could hardly be flatter,
Surrounded by wind-drifts of old reading matter—

The disciplined craftsman had no choice but to surrender. Yet he resisted to the end the ways in which his aged body betrayed the reaches of his mind.

Between the lines of *The Devils and Canon Barham*

one can discern this struggle. His essays are on "poets,
novelists and monsters." His few pages on Hemingway
are "pure" Edmund Wilson—the documentation, the anal-
ysis, the cross-examination, the high summary, the "glint-
ing exactness," as V. S. Pritchett puts it. Many fat books
have been written about Ernest Hemingway; but Wilson's
essay may well be the last judicial word on the subject.
The poets of this volume are Pound and his editing of
Eliot; the novelists, in addition to Hemingway, are the
English amateur, Maurice Baring, who like Edmund was
at home in Russian letters, and two from America's literary
backyard, Henry Blake Fuller and Harold Frederic. Edmund Wilson liked to define such minor talents who
wrought so much and so hard for so little, and remain
locked now in a kind of drab literary past. He inserted also
an excellent essay on Mencken. As for the "monsters,"
they are related to the violent and eerie *Ingoldsby Legends*
and the vivid Canon Barham who created them, for Wilson was always challenged by sado-masochism and the
nightmare world. And then there is a very last piece, a
travelogue on the monster-statues of Bomarzo, where we
feel the essayist's fascination, and yet see him faltering and
tired: he can no longer push his prose hard enough, yet
he can still be interested, and passionately curious, at the
devious forms of the human imagination.

Some readers may find particular pleasure in a fragment
of a novel begun in collaboration with Edwin O'Connor.
It is about a magician named Baldini and it reflects not
only Wilson's ancient interest in stage magic, but his love
for any form of "entertainment." Thus he embarked on a
kind of Arabian Nights tale with his neighborly novelist
and fellow-magician at Wellfleet, the author of *The Last
Hurrah*. One can see the project as a collision, rather than
a collaboration. Outwardly they plotted and planned; in-
wardly creative devils took over. They wrote alternate

chapters. It got to be a collaboration of "upmanship"; each
trumped the other's chapter. It could only end in deadlock
—and it did. Moreover it was a story of two magicians who
think of collaborating on stage but whose egos are too
strong. Thus the writers acted out a kind of vaudeville,
"Edmund and Edwin," in which fiction was fact, fact
fiction.

Of great importance is Wilson's vigorous polemical essay
on the editing of modern editions of American authors.
During all his years, he bubbled with impatience over the
way in which professors write books not out of love of
letters, or out of curiosity and joy, but simply to "publish
or perish." He criticized even so well-known a figure as
Harvard's F. O. Matthiessen for standing in front of a
given text, instead of behind it, where scholars belong. He
felt strongly that modern writing need not be edited in the
way scholars edit Chaucer of Shakespeare; and that posthumous works in particular must not be subjected to "the
academic mania of exactly reproducing texts." His essay
devoted to the Modern Language Association's elaborate
yet somehow irrelevant quest for variorum readings in
American authors (with much talk that belongs to the
proof room rather than the scholarly library) should—and
will—trouble the conscience of American and English
studies in years to come. There is much more to be said
about this; and much more about the high qualities of
Wilson's developed style, and his constant war against the
pedantries and hermeticism of modern critics. He was
himself the most *disinterested* of critics, in the fine old
sense of the word—that is the most objective. He refused to
use criticism for anything but honest inquiry: he wanted
always to discover the truth of personality, the nature of
expression, the self-revealing qualities of genius or talent,
or even mediocrity. Each essay of Edmund Wilson's is a
voyage into literary history, biography, criticism, society:

and a demonstration to the prolix and the half-hearted that
writing is a stern discipline.

In the verses I have quoted, Edmund Wilson mentioned
that he had pinned above his desk, for encouragement, "a
high tonic slogan I stole from the Torah." This was one
way of fighting age and "sloth." I suppose Hebrew, after
Russian, was the language at which he worked hardest. It
had disturbed him long ago to find in the library he inherited from a clerical ancestor an Old Testament in a
language he could not read, and he had enrolled with the
young at the Princeton Theological Seminary to overcome
the gap. A visitor to the quiet New England graveyard, to
the isolated grave of Edmund Wilson (which I saw when
the ground was hard and the trees bare in the Cape Cod
winter blueness) can read the "tonic slogan"—the three
Hebrew words, which his widow, Elena, had carved into
the headstone:

חזק חזק ונתחזק

"Be strong, be strong, grow in strength." The sorcerer is
thus buried under Holy Writ: readers of the Old Testament are enjoined, in this call for strength, not only to
endure, but to grow stronger that they may return and
read anew the Word of God. It was perhaps not by chance
that Edmund Wilson found solace in the ancient admonition in his Presbyterian grandfather's bible. All literature
seemed to him to possess some divine illumination, and
these pages show how he harbored his strength, how he
read, and reread, wrote, and rewrote—almost to the end.

Honolulu, January 1973

# THE DEVILS
# AND CANON BARHAM

# THE DEVILS AND CANON BARHAM

There is one book that I read in my childhood for which I still have a kind of fetishistic feeling: Richard Harris Barham's *The Ingoldsby Legends*. I keep copies in both my winter and my summer houses, and in the former have a small collection of books by and about Barham. When I recently became aware that the *Legends* was missing from my summer place, in which I had had only one copy, and that I did not know what had happened to it, I was uneasy until, in the following year, it was returned by a friend to whom I had lent it. It had been my grandfather's edition (New York, 1884), from which he had read to his children. The *Legends* was once immensely popular. Of an English "People's Edition" of a hundred thousand copies that sold in 1881 for sixpence, more than sixty thousand went off on the day of publication. Between 1857 and 1864, it had run through twenty-three editions; the secondhand bookstores of London and Edinburgh, of New York and Boston, are full of old discarded copies. Yet one hardly ever hears of it nowadays. Compton Mackenzie and Anthony Powell have mentioned it in their novels, and Ronald Knox wrote a very short tribute, which is included in his *Literary Distractions*. But the only at all adequate account of Barham's writings that I have ever seen is in the second of George Saintsbury's three volumes of *Essays in English Literature*. Saintsbury says that he can recite half the legends by heart, and if one is exposed to them early in life, one is likely to find it hard to forget them. Richard Barham was a genuine poet, who exerts a peculiar spell. A man of some property in Kent, a minor canon of St. Paul's Cathedral, an amateur but learned antiquary, he wrote mainly to amuse himself, and his verse has a spontaneity of unexpected rhyming and reckless imagination that makes it different from anybody else's. (It is possible that the legends were partly derived from the versified *Tales* of Praed, which also season the romantic with the comic, and have also, to a lesser extent, their interfering devils, but Praed is more polite, less boisterous, and usually much less effective.)

The *Legends* was also fortunate in its illustrators. The illustrations are one of the features which once made it so attractive to young people. I especially recommend the three-volume Bentley edition of 1894 (the eighty-eighth), edited by Barham's daughter and annotated by his son-in-law, with all the steel engravings and woodcuts of Leech, Cruikshank, Thackeray, Tenniel, and du Maurier. Any drawings later than these seem to me quite inappropriate. I had, nevertheless, on the wall of my room at prep school the colored pictures from a contemporary Ingoldsby calendar—which shows that a familiarity with the legends must still in 1912 have persisted in England—but these never appeared to me authentic, and when I later saw the fairy-tale drawings by Arthur Rackham (of 1907), I rejected them with indignation. One of the beauties of the edition mentioned above is the frontispiece to the first volume, in George Cruikshank's very best vein: the smooth-faced and apparently eupeptic Reverend Barham tranquilly writing at his table with something like a smile of ironic enjoyment, while his publisher, Richard Bentley, evidently kneeling at his elbow, spies anxiously on his work through what used to be called a quizzing-glass, one hand raised as if in shocked alarm, while the best known of Barham's characters, the Jackdaw of Rheims, disheveled and scrawny from the Cardinal's curse, stands on the table before him, and behind, above, and all about him rises a tapestry of demons and bugaboos, the tumult of bristling and phantasmal beings which this pleasant-humored cleric has evoked—the witches with their spitting black cat and their broomstick turned into a weapon, the hysterical Mousquetaire guarded on either side by his real and his phantom nurse, the goggle-eyed skeleton drummer, the florid and terrified monks, the vision of St. Ermengarde with her scowl and her menacing palm branch, and, crouching in the lower right-hand corner, at the base of all this fearsome phantasmagoria, the key spirit, the black, brutish Devil, with his trap of ferocious white teeth and his writhing, impatient tail.

I was therefore extremely eager, when I saw a biography of Barham announced—*Richard Harris Barham*, by William G. Lane, the first since a memoir by Barham's son—to read it and use it as a pretext for writing about this now forgotten favorite of the English-speaking world. What a dampening disappointment it has proved to be! Mr. Lane is a conventional professor at the University of Colorado, and his biography is a typical product of the American academic mill. It reads as though it had been undertaken, with no genuine interest in its subject and no feeling for the period in which Barham lived, as the performance of an available academic job, not hitherto performed by anyone else, which would earn academic credit. Mr. Lane has done the proper research, he has had access to unpublished material. I am indebted to him for figures and dates, but the value of his study stops there. His pages are almost always ankle-deep, and sometimes up to their necks, in footnotes, but these notes, as well as much of the text, record facts of no interest whatever. We get a good deal more information about the history of the periodicals in which Barham's writings appeared, and other uninteresting matters, than about the writer's personal life or his contribution to English literature. One chapter of thirty-six pages—called "The Primitive Muse of Thomas Ingoldsby"—in a book of 260 pages is all the attention Lane gives to Barham's only claim to remembrance. One questions the usefulness, for example, of a footnote explaining that Lord Albert Conyngham, the leader of a schism in the British Archaeological Association—"(1805–1860): See D N B"—whose side Richard Barham supported, was "created Lord Londesborough in 1849. In that year, also, he led a faction that severed connection with the Archaeological Association. Later he became vice-president of the Archaeological Institute and president of the London and Middlesex Archaeological Society in 1855." This person has no relevance at all to the career of Richard Barham, and if anyone is curious about him he can always, as Mr. Lane suggests, consult the British Dictionary of National Biography—which the non-scholarly reader may not be able to recognize from Mr. Lane's abbreviation. There are many inches and pages of this sort of thing. For whom, one asks, is such a book written? For what market has it been produced? The answers are that it seems to have been written exclusively in order to fill the requirements—among the chief of which are heavy layers of footnotes and authentic original research—of the American Ph.D. thesis, and that no identifiable public is supposed to read it: it is simply to stand as a block in the building of an academic reputation.

It is so much, in fact, a book for nobody that we cannot always be sure whether the author really knows what he is talking about or whether he assumes his readers are so much at home in the period that they do not have to have things explained. He mentions "Titmarsh," for instance, without explaining that it is a pseudonym of Thackeray's, and he may take it for granted that the reader will know. But is he himself aware that the verses of Barham's quoted at length on pages 64–6 are a parody of a once well-known poem by George Canning about the University of Göttingen? Does he know that Barham's reference in some verses on page 98 to Aristophanes's theory of the origin of the sexes is to what was propounded not in one of Aristophanes's plays but in the *Symposium* of Plato by his character of Aristophanes? Mr. Lane does not take the trouble to explain why he thinks "it is necessary to view with suspicion whatever [John Payne] Collier offers in the way of 'newly discovered' or 'hitherto unpublished' manuscripts." Is it simply because he is sure that the professor who reads his thesis will know that John Collier was a forger of manuscripts and that he does not expect that anyone else will ever read what he is writing? If there are to be so many footnotes, some of them might well be used to elucidate these matters. It is certain that Mr. Lane does not know very well his period or his author —that is, know them in the sense that he has been able imaginatively to enter into the life of the one or to appreciate the work of the other. Barham was so much a part of a certain London milieu, with its thick and riotous atmosphere of semi-bohemian clubs, the Beefsteak and the Garrick, of smoke and wine and outrageous jokes and gossip, that he ought to be shown in this atmosphere. But Lane's biography can only dispel it. He does include a bleak enough chapter called "The Livelier London Days," and he has earlier made some effort to explain the peculiar prestige of Barham's special friend Theodore Hook, but he does not succeed in giving any real impression of this more or less professional entertainer who set the tone of the humor of the period by a series of popular novels and whose comic improvisations of operas were a great feature of uproarious evenings. He does not seem to understand exactly who and what were such other characteristic figures as "Father Prout" and William Maginn and John Forster: learned, convivial men, eccentric or underbred or careless of their literary gifts, the first an expelled Jesuit, best known for his poem "The Bells of Shandon," who amused himself by translating English poems into Greek and Latin, French and Italian, and pretending that the originals were plagiarisms; the second, also a classicist, the perfect type of the drunken Irish journalist who displays intermittent brilliance; and the third called by Barham "a low scribbler and without an atom of talent and totally un- used to the society of gentlemen," but the friend and bi- ographer of Dickens, who is said to have used him in the creation of Podsnap, in *Our Mutual Friend*—the perfect pompous Victorian father, always fearful of the possibility of "bringing a blush into the cheek of the young person."

All this world, so much stripped and chilled and robbed of its peculiar flavors in Mr. Lane's academic exercise, is brought to life in the diaries and letters of Dalton Bar- ham's memoir of his father—*The Life and Letters of the Rev. Richard Harris Barham,* with its humorous rhymes and anecdotes, its practical jokes and conundrums, its ghost stories and stag dinners. (I have used the two- volume version published in 1870.) If anyone at this date should doubt that the London of Dickens once existed, this book, the record of a writer of quite different opin- ions and interests from Dickens's, will confirm the picture left by the novelist. Though Richard Barham was on good terms with Dickens, his politics were entirely conservative,

and he evidently did not approve of the tendencies of
Dickens's novels; he complains of "a sort of Radicalish
tone about *Oliver Twist* which I don't altogether like."
(Mr. Lane seems to second the suggestion of another
scholar that "the irreverent clergyman in Chapter V of
*Oliver Twist* may have originated in [an] underlying resentment." But in this chapter the only reference to a
clergyman is in a single brief paragraph, which mentions
an unnamed cleric as skimping the burial service of a
pauper. Does some other text exist?)

Yet in the younger Barham's chronicle of his father's
life, all the horrors of the London of the period are present: the epidemics of scarlatina, influenza, and cholera;
the lives of destitution and crime which Dickens brought
before his readers. Canon Barham did the best he could
for the miserable people of his parish: he got money for a
"distressed author" whom he found in a badly furnished,
unheated room, with his wife sitting on a tub as she tried
to nurse a dying child. This woman was afraid that her
child would die without being baptized, and Barham ad-
ministered the sacrament. In the case of the wife and
children of a "resurrection man," when the husband had
been hanged for the murder of an Italian boy whose body
he had sold to doctors for dissection, Barham furnished
them with recommendations—the wife had worked for
one of Barham's parishioners—at a time when women and
children mistaken for the family had been attacked in the
streets. He and his wife had suffered many afflictions. His
right arm had been shattered at the age of thirteen when
a Dover mail coach turned over; and the Barhams had lost
five of their children—one boy, who had given promise
of brilliance, had died in his thirteenth year, and his death
remained a lasting grief. Another son died of cholera in
twenty-four hours. Mrs. Barham, who had survived a lifetime of constant childbearing and child-rearing, died, her

son tells us, after "six years of unceasing and at times almost unendurable suffering" caused by some ailment of the eye. One feels all through *The Ingoldsby Legends*, for all the rattling jollity of the verse, an uneasiness of danger and pain. It is partly this undercurrent that gives the book its power. The compensation for the hardships of the time was the life of conviviality on which the Canon's letters and journals so constantly dwell: the dinners of port wine and punch that ended in topical songs, in burlesque impersonations and conundrums, the charades and the tableaux vivants, the inexhaustible humorous anecdotes about Lord M—— and the Duke of Sussex, about popular writers and actors and the amusing Scotch and Irish peasantry. As in Dickens, the rude jokes and the cheerful glass drown the Marshalsea and Newgate in the background. "This elasticity of spirit," writes Barham in a letter, "which, in spite of nature herself, as it were, will rebound under pressure is one, and not the least, of God's blessings. That I do not encourage, but fight up against gloomy thoughts, you will see in the 'Mousquetaire,' a legend I am finishing for Bentley. The fact is I find work my best solace, and I do work incessantly, though I fear not to the same purpose as I think I could have done had my poor boy lived for me to have worked for"—though this "Black Mousquetaire" which is keeping him busy is itself a tale of morbid obsession. The note of the period is sounded in Barham's account of the funeral of Dicky Suett, a popular low comedian, who was famous for playing clowns, at which one of the mourners provoked laughter from tears by imitating the voice of the dead man: "Aha! Jemmy—O la! I'm going to be buried! O la! O lawk! O dear!"

A rereading of *The Ingoldsby Legends* reveals the conflicting impulses in the mind of Richard Barham. All that I know that has been written about him has been occupied mainly with his grotesque imagination and with his skill in unconventional rhyming. In this latter capacity, as has sometimes been said, he was not inferior to Byron or Browning. He could, with apparently perfect readiness, toss off two- and three-syllable rhymes which one could not possibly have predicted—resorting, if necessary, to Latin or French pronounced in the English fashion. (Father Knox, in his paper on the *Legends,* explains that this trick is easier than it looks: "You produce the far-fetched, the composite, the improbable rhyme *first,* and when its more reputable fellow appears at a suitable interval, the reader's ear is tickled by the occurrence of something inevitable.") Barham was gifted with some special genius which makes his meters and rhyming as catching as music, so that they run in your head after reading. But he exercises also another special spell, which I have not seen commemorated—a spell which is half diabolical. A fundamental feature of his *Legends* is the ever-reviving vitality and the ultimate invincibility of the Devil. In some of the interpolated prose pieces, which are written in the old-fashioned pompous-facetious style and in which the rapid juggling of the verse and the frequent distracting digressions do not come between the reader and the story, one is troubled by the fact that the victims of the invisible evil forces—the girl in the "Singular Passage in the Life of the Late Henry Harris, D.D.," the gardener in "Jerry Jarvis's Wig"—are quite innocent of any sin, that they do not deserve, in the one case, to be tortured to death at long distance by two young medical students practicing the black arts, one of them her fiancé, and, in the other, to be bewitched by a similar evil agent from a perfectly honest man into a robber and murderer who ends on the gallows. It should be noted that in such cases as these there is never any final explanation of even a plausibly fantastic kind of what has happened and why. Barham's novel *My Cousin Nicholas* is a full-scale development of this theme of the gratuitously diabolical. Cousin Nicholas is a horrid

young man, unscrupulously malicious and impudent, not
unlike an Evelyn Waugh character, whose life is devoted
to practical jokes on a more and more cruel and more and
more disastrous scale. He has not one sympathetic trait.
He is a spirit of perversity whom Barham has raised and
who eventually seems to get out of hand. The story had
been suggested by a youthful prank of Barham's father,
who had stolen a magnificent and much-cherished brass
knocker from the front door of his father's house. The son
had declined to live with him, had set himself up in a
bachelor's establishment, and had offended the older Barham so seriously that the latter cut him out of his will and
for two years refused to see him. This incident occurs in
the novel, but in the novel it is only the precursor of a
series of so much worse offenses that the author at one
point confesses in a letter to finding himself in perplexity
as to how to get rid of Nicholas: "He begins to embarrass
me cruelly. Like *Mr. Puff* in the *Critic*, I have got him
on the stage, and how to get him off again with decency
Heavens knows. He cannot, any more than Sheridan's
heroes, make his 'exit praying'; and whether to break his
neck out of a balloon, or blow him up in a powder-mill
at Dartford, I am really, for the present, at a loss to determine." What he finally decided upon was to have Cousin
Nicholas shot by someone who had reason for hating him,
at a moment when the infernal young man was getting
ready to rob and even perhaps to murder his father.

This spirit of malignant mischief is present all through
the *Legends*. The three little devils of "The Truants," who
have escaped "from the National School below," are de-
fying their Mentor himself, and one is so insubordinate
that he never goes back to Hell. The Devil is always
erupting, and though the saints usually succeed in curb-
ing him, it is sometimes a near thing. In the case of those
devils who, in "The Lay of Saint Cuthbert," have, in a
moment of profane fury, been invited to dinner by Sir

Guy Le Scroope, the victim himself of a malicious hoax on the part of one of his friends, who has contrived that the guests shall not come, St. Cuthbert, in rescuing Sir Guy's little son, with whom the devils are playing catch, is nevertheless so little confident as to how far his authority extends that he is forced to make a kind of deal with them by allowing them to remain and gobble up the dinner.

Closely allied with this diabolic element is the gruesomeness of many of the stories. You have, in "The Auto-da-Fé," a description of Jews being burned alive, and, in "Bloudie Jack of Shrewsberrie," an English Bluebeard who saves carefully, tied up in clusters, the ring fingers and great toes of his murdered brides and who is finally torn to pieces by the populace. "I never liked the story," Barham wrote to a woman friend, "which is so very *nursery* a one, and was all but forced upon me." He does not say who forced it upon him, but he cannot really have needed much persuasion. There is a good deal of decapitation and dismemberment in the *Legends*. "The Ingoldsby Penance" and "The Legend of Hamilton Tighe" both involve apparitions that carry their severed heads. In the case of the latter of these, Mr. Lane quotes someone as writing to Barham, "Suffice it to state, what my friend Miss Mitford can confirm, that the simple recitation of 'Hamilton Tighe' has actually made persons start and turn pale, and complain of nervous excitement." In "A Lay of St. Gengulphus," the later-to-be-canonized hero, whose wife had been having an affair with "a spruce young spark of a Learned Clerk" while Gengulphus was off on a pilgrimage to the Holy Land, is, as soon as he returns, smothered and methodically cut into pieces by them; but his head, which has been thrown down a well, is pulled up by a maid in a pail of water, and a resuscitated Gengulphus, reassembling his arms and legs, puts in an astounding appearance at a banquet given by the Prince

Bishop. There is a mention in this connection of a contemporary London murder in which a cabinetmaker and
his mistress had dismembered another woman, and the
bad taste of this topical reference was one of the points
made by Richard Hengist Horne, the author of that long-
sunken epic *Orion,* in an attack on *The Ingoldsby Legends.* But Barham had gone further and followed "Gengulphus" with another grim tale connected with the
hanging of this cabinetmaker. "The Execution: A Sporting Anecdote," supposed to be based on an actual incident, tells the story of how My Lord Tomnoddy, with
three of his debauched companions, hires a room for the
night at the Magpie and Stump tavern, opposite the Old
Bailey prison, in order to be sure of having a good view of
the hanging which is to take place in the morning; but
as the result of a night spent in drunken revelry, they go
to sleep and do not awaken till the execution is over and
the body has been cut down and taken away. This, they
realize, will make them a laughingstock, but they cannot
do anything about it; even swells in their exalted position
cannot have the man hanged again. Perhaps the most
repellent of the *Legends* is the one called "The Knight
and the Lady: A Domestic Legend of the Reign of Queen
Anne," with its epigraph attributed to "Thomson—or
Somebody": "Hail, wedded love! mysterious tie!" A handsome Lady Jane is married to a shortsighted and tottering
Sir Thomas. He falls into a pond on his place in an attempt to capture a tadpole. He is drowned, and his body,
half eaten by eels, is discovered only some time after. In
the meantime—a kind of thing that is frequent in the Ingoldsby world—Lady Jane has consoled herself with the
comradeship of an attractive young captain. She and her
lover make an excellent supper on the eels found still
clinging to the body, at the end of which Lady Jane ob-
serves, "with a pensive air":

To Thompson, the valet, while taking away,
When supper was over, the cloth and the tray,—
              "Eels a many
              I've ate; but any
     So good ne'er tasted before!—
They're a fish, too, of which I'm remarkably fond.
Go—pop Sir Thomas again in the Pond—
Poor dear!—HE'LL CATCH US SOME MORE!!"

The author of the *Legends* was reprimanded, as I learn
from Mr. Lane, by Horne, in the essay mentioned above,
called "Poison in Jest," for his incorrigible "hideous lev-
ity," which was sure to have a "bad influence"—I quote
from Mr. Lane's paraphrase—"on the younger generation,
which was bad enough without such assistance." "Where-
fore," concluded Horne, "an iron hand is now laid upon
the shoulder of Thomas Ingoldsby, and a voice murmurs
in his ear, 'Brother!—no more of this!'"

But to isolate this element in *The Ingoldsby Legends*
would be rather to misrepresent them. The murders and
mutilations, the ordeals and the outrages of life are real,
but it is possible to laugh about them. So all-enveloping,
in fact, is Barham's atmosphere of rollicking abandon that
it is somewhat surprising to re-examine the Legends and
take account of the unpleasantness of their subjects. It is
significant, perhaps, that the most popular of them has
always been "The Jackdaw of Rheims"—of which Barham
said in a letter to his editor that it was "struck off at a
heat and almost in despair, when I found it impossible to
finish the other article in time," and of which, in writing
to a friend, he expressed the unwarranted fear that "the
poor 'Jackdaw' will be sadly pecked at. Had I more time, I
meant to have engrafted on it a story I have heard Can-
non tell of a magpie of his acquaintance." The "Jackdaw,"
however, owes its special popularity, undoubtedly, to its

simplicity and brevity, and also, I think, to its assimila-
bility as one of the few of the legends that have nothing
to shock mid-Victorian sensibilities, to its involving no
malicious perversity that could embarrass the cheerful
reader. The Cardinal's ring is stolen, and the Cardinal
does not know that it is his pet bird who has stolen it.
He lays on the thief a terrible curse, which is to blight
him in every possible situation. When the poor little bird
turns up, he is horribly racked and deplumed, and the
Cardinal must take off the curse and try to make him
amends by reinstating him in even more than his previous
favor—which, however, the poet, with his cynical touch,
lets us know made him rather obnoxious. The jackdaw
dies "in the odour of sanctity":

> When, as words were too faint His merits to paint,
> The Conclave determined to make him a Saint;
> And on newly-made Saints and Popes, as you know,
> It's the custom, at Rome, new names to bestow,
> So they canonised him by the name of Jem Crow!

An entirely satisfactory ending, with no hanging and no
lasting humiliation—though the instinct to punish cruelly
as a penalty for moral turpitude has been carelessly in-
dulged by the Cardinal. There thus finds expression in
*The Ingoldsby Legends* a feeling both horrified and mischievous for the constant misfortunes of life, together
with the impulse to make fun of them, to banish their
horror from one's mind, as the song and the bottle go
round, or as one sits at one's table in tranquillity reeling
out one's amusing verse. These crimes and these acci-
dents would cause us to shudder if we were not consoled
by the poet's high spirits and left with gay rhymes and
rhythms reverberating in our heads.

Richard Barham, not long before his death, composed,

in "As I Laye A-Thynkynge," an archaized but oddly moving poem which has haunted the minds of his posthumous readers as much as any of his comic pieces. A "noble Knyghte" goes off with a light, cheerful heart to the war, then is seen lying dead, his steed running away with broken rein; a "lovely Mayde" and her lover are seen, then the maid is tearing her hair "in sad despaire," evidently deserted by the lover; a "lovely Childe" is smiling at his father, then is seen pale in death. All the time a bird is singing, at first merrily but afterward sadly:

> As I laye a-thynkynge, her meaning was exprest:
> "Follow, follow me away,
> It boots not to delay,"
> 'Twas so she seemed to saye,
> "Here is Rest!"

Barham also wrote some verses to his dead daughter, these rather undistinguished, and some fragments of a queer ballad of which his son says that "the tone was to have been graver and the subject more pathetic than that of most of his stories." It is about a "Radiant Boy," who is apparently trying to come back to the earth from the other world of the dead. A living boy who can see him, although he is invisible to everybody else, is given the name Tom Ingoldsby, the pseudonym under which to the end Richard Barham published all of these comic writings, thus disassociating the conscientious priest from the products of his frequently profane and sometimes bawdy imagination. But this lyric, "As I Laye A-Thynkynge," and his still often anthologized "Epigram" on Horace's *"Eheu fugaces"* remain, in their characteristically whimsical forms, as his valedictories to his readers.

November 21, 1970

# TWO NEGLECTED AMERICAN NOVELISTS

## I. Henry B. Fuller: The Art
## of Making It Flat

The nineties and the early 1900's, when looked at from the later decades, are likely to seem a dim period in American literature. The quality and the content of the fiction were mainly determined by the magazines that aimed to please a feminine public. There were writers of great reputation whom no one except the literary historian would think of looking into today. But there did exist also—outsold and outpublicized—a kind of underground of real social critics and conscientious artists who were hardly recognized or who were recognized only when one of them struck off some book that was daring or arresting enough to call special attention to its author. Harold Frederic's *The Damnation of Theron Ware,* which dealt in a disturbing way with the contemporary problems of the clergy, was a book that was much read both in England and here; Stephen Crane's *The Red Badge of Courage* was so intensely conceived and written that, though pooh-poohed by academics like Barrett Wendell, it could not be disregarded, and Crane himself became a public legend, although every effort was made to see that this legend was a disreputable one; George W. Cable, in the eighties, had had his success with a serious novel, *The Grandissimes,* but his treatment of situations created in the South by the mixture of white and black blood and his pamphleteering books on the Negro question became so repugnant to his editors and so outrageous to his Southern neighbors that he was forced to fall back on sentimental romance and exploitation of the then marketable "local color"; Kate Chopin, who wrote also of Louisiana, was also acceptable as a local-colorist, but she so scandalized the public in 1899 by her treatment of adultery in *The Awakening* that she is said to have been discouraged from writing any more novels; and, in spite of the championship of Howells, the New Englander John DeForest, in his Balzacian effort to cover his own era as well as parts of the historical past—the Revolution and the Salem witches, the Civil War and the corruption of the Grant administration—in an objective and realistic way, was never accepted at all.

It has been only in quite recent years that this area has been gradually excavated. The first collection of Crane, who died in 1900, was brought out in 1925, in a very limited edition. DeForest's *Miss Ravenel's Conversion,* his most notable Civil War novel, was reprinted only in 1939, *The Grandissimes* only in 1957. *The Damnation of Theron Ware* has suddenly been resuscitated in no less than three recent reprintings, and Frederic's stories of the Civil War have now for the first time been collected in one volume. The latest of these writers to be discovered and the one who has in general had least justice done him is Henry B. Fuller, but now at last *With the Procession,* one of the best of his novels, has been reprinted, and this provides an occasion to give some account of Fuller, a unique and distinguished writer who does not deserve to be dumped in the drawer devoted to regional novelists for a chapter in an academic literary history.

Henry Blake Fuller was born in Chicago (January 9, 1857), but his family on both sides had been New Englanders. His grandfather was a cousin of Margaret Fuller. This grandfather, following a frequent progression, had moved first to western New York, then to the Middle West. He was one of those Americans of the period who combined making money in business with a sense of public responsibility. He had been a dry-goods merchant in Albion, New York, a county judge in Michigan, and in still-pioneering Chicago a railroad man and the entrepreneur of the laying of forty miles of water pipes.

Henry was an only son. At school he was a brilliant student. He did not go to college but had all the New England will to self-improvement. He learned languages and studied music, composed, wrote poetry, kept a diary, and made lists of necessary reading. He led a protected and isolated life, saw little of other young people. Out of school, he worked at first in his father's bank, but when Henry was twenty-two, Judge Fuller died, and he probably left his grandson some money, for Henry sailed for Europe that summer. He traveled in Europe a year, and thereafter, through the eighties and nineties, continued every few years to return for six months or so.

The first result of these visits, published in 1890, under a pseudonym and at Fuller's own expense, was a short novel, *The Chevalier of Pensieri-Vani*. This book, which was called in its time a little classic and a minor masterpiece, became the object of a kind of cult, of which I believe the last representative was the late Carl Van Vechten. It is an account of the travels in Italy of a cultivated Italian gentleman and is something of an actual travel book in the taste of the then frequent articles in the more serious magazines, with their drawings of Old Chester and Picturesque Tuscany, intended especially for ladies who were obliged to stay at home or who saved up to and

looked forward to eventual trips. But it is also something
other than this. It is diversified by little adventures and
flavored with demure humor. *The Chevalier*—which soon
went into a better edition, published under Fuller's own
name—was the first of a series of novels all preserving the
same tone and dealing with the same group of characters.
The names of these characters alone will convey Fuller's
playful humor: besides the Cavaliere himself, there are
his friend the French Seigneur of Hors-Concours; the
Swiss Chatelaine of La Trinité and her companion Miss
Aurelia West of Ohio, who later marries a Lyon manufacturer and becomes Mme. la Comtesse Aurélie de Feu-
illevolante; the Duke of Avon and Severn; Baron Zeitgeist
and the Freiherr von Kaltenau; the Prorege of Arcopia
and the Marquis of Tempo-Rubato; and Mr. Occident,
also from Ohio. The second of these books, *The Chatelaine of La Trinité,* appeared in 1892, but Fuller did not
follow these up till *The Last Refuge,* of 1900, and did not
conclude the series till 1929, when, just before the end of
his life, he published *Gardens of This World.* These books
belong to a school that is nowadays of little interest. The
then fashionable stories of Americans encountering sophisticated Europeans, usually embellished by titles, have today become rather embarrassing. They are one of the
symptoms of the longing to get away from the ugly and
crass society that flourished after the Civil War. Americans then had a mania for looking up their family trees
and trying to establish connections with some noble house
in England or elsewhere. Henry James had his Passionate
Pilgrim, Mark Twain his American Claimant. At its gaud-
iest, this dream produced Graustark, the imaginary Balkan
kingdom of glamour, dashing deeds, and gallant romance
which was created by George Barr McCutcheon, originally a farm boy from Indiana.

A more alembicated product was the late fiction of

Henry Harland, a coy kind of fairy tales—marvels of American snobbery and syrupy *fin-de-siècle* fine writing—which, so popular in the early 1900's, are ridiculous, though still readable, today. The enchanting young hero and heroine, conversing in well-bred banter, are either royal or of very high rank, which, in their willingness to fall in love with commoners, they implausibly manage to conceal till they are headed for the final embrace. Harland's *The Cardinal's Snuffbox*, once thought so utterly delightful and the author's greatest success, is actually so absurd that when the editor of *Punch,* Owen Seaman, attempted to parody it in his book *Borrowed Plumes,* he could only fall short of the original. Edgar Saltus, the New York "society" novelist, is also in this tradition, but a man of real worldly experience, he is genuinely amusing and witty, and he cultivated a certain perversity which prevented him from becoming saccharine as it prevented him from being popular. The European novels of Fuller belong to this tradition, too, but though they are not so wicked as Saltus's, they are very much more intelligent and much better written than Harland's. And Fuller, who so loved his noble connoisseurs, with their self-assured Old World savoir-faire, is nevertheless drolly ironic about those Americans themselves who admired and exaggerated these qualities. The happiest episode in the series seems to me the account of the efforts of Miss West of Ohio to induce the Chatelaine of La Trinité to live up to her ancestry and social position, which she has always taken for granted and to which she has not given much thought, and to arrange matches for her with suitable men, none of whom are much interested in her. The Chatelaine herself loses interest in the operation and retires to a house of retreat in Lausanne. In *Gardens of This World,* which is supposed to take place after the First World War, these characters, now grown old, are still wandering around Europe, still in search of charming quiet spots, but they everywhere encounter Americans—a millionaire who wants to buy up ruins and works of art and transport them to the United States, but also two adventurous and energetic boys who are interested in flying and one of whom (he is half French, the son of Feuille-volante) eventually goes into his father's business.

For, in spite of Fuller's regret at the decline of Europe and his harsh or sad criticisms of his own country, there was a strong strain of patriotism in him, even a feeling of loyalty to Chicago. In the intervals between his trips abroad, he had always had to return to his native city, where, after his father's death in 1885, he took over the responsibilities of the family's business affairs. In those of his books that take place in Europe, one is impressed by the thoroughness and exactitude of his knowledge of history, geography, literature, art, and architecture. He was equally well informed about Chicago. He seems always to have been up-to-date on the streets, the population, the buildings, on new developments and organizations. The objection sometimes made to Henry James that he knew nothing about American business is not at all in order in the case of the part-time expatriate Fuller. He knew everything about the interests which he had to administer—industry, real estate, finance, and the legal procedures entailed by these. In connection with the family properties, he collected rents and checked on the buildings; he could even himself mend the plumbing and complained that this took up too much of his time. And he now began to write about Chicago. The results of this were rather surprising. The precision and elegance of Fuller's style—so unusual in the United States of the nineties—really make a better showing here, because they lend a distinction to often crude material, than they do in the European books, where they still leave a little arid, a little bleak with accu-

rate fact, material which the author has labored to render
graceful and alluring and foreign. In his travels, he is not
very far from the tinted impressionism of Henry James,
which seems to emanate from his mind like a vapor.

Fuller now writes two novels—*The Cliff-Dwellers*
(1893) and *With the Procession* (1895)—about the life
of the new, energetic city. The first of these dramatizes
the organism of an eighteen-story office building, the Clifton—the man who built it and the people who work in it;
the second the fortunes of a family of more or less simple
Western origins (the father is a well-to-do wholesale
grocer) who, as the city grows and prospers, are unable
to adjust themselves to its more and more accelerated
progress and, borne along by the money-driven tide which
is symbolized in the first pages by the traffic of a Chicago
street, become bewildered and broken in their efforts to
keep up "with the procession." The general situation is
embodied in the figure of the rich Mrs. Granger Bates,
compelled by reason of her money to try to live up to a
high position and to occupy a grand mansion, but reduced
by her homely tastes to reconstituting a kind of inner
sanctuary in the image of the snug and vulgar home of
her youth. The author has summed up in these novels
both his intimate observation of Chicago and his half-
alien criticism of it. There is the overpowering faith of the
Chicagoans in the future of their new city: "Individually,
we may be of a rather humble grade of atoms," he makes
one of the men in *The Cliff-Dwellers* say, "but we are
crystallizing into a compound that is going to exercise a
tremendous force. . . . You may have seen the boiling
of the kettle, but you have hardly seen the force that
feeds the flame. The big buildings are all well enough,
and the big crowds in the streets, and the reports of the
banks and railways and the Board of Trade. But there is
something, now, beyond and behind all that. . . . Does

it seem unreasonable that the State which produced the two greatest figures of the greatest epoch in our history, and which has done most within the last ten years to check alien excesses and un-American ideas, should also be the State to give the country the final blend of the American character and its ultimate metropolis?" "His wife sat beside him silent, but with her hand on his," adds Fuller, "and when he answered, she pressed it meaningly; for to the Chicagoan—even the middle-aged female Chicagoan—the name of the town, in its formal, ceremonial use, has a power that no other word in the language quite possesses. It is a shibboleth, as regards its pronunciation; it is a trumpet call, as regards its effect. It has all the electrifying and unifying power of a college yell." And there is the social insecurity of Chicagoans: "Commercially, we feel our own footing; socially, we are rather abashed by the pretensions that any new arrival chooses to make. We are a little afraid of him, and, to tell the truth, we are a little afraid of each other." Fuller is able, from his knowledge of Europe, to understand the beginnings of gangsterism, which, with the increase of immigrant workers, is already manifesting itself as an unruly and dangerous element: "The populations of Italy and Poland and Hungary," says one of the characters in *With the Procession,* "what view now do *they* take of the government—their government, all government? Isn't it an implacable and immemorial enemy—a great and cruel and dreadful monster to be evaded, hoodwinked, combated, stabbed in the dark if occasion offers? . . . Is it an easy matter, on their coming over here, to make them feel themselves a part of [the government], and to imbue them with a loyalty to it?" One of the features of both these books is the figure, which was to become so familiar in the American fiction of this period, of the extravagant and socially ambitious woman who drives and sometimes ruins her hard-working husband. In *The Cliff-Dwellers*, the power behind everything, the wife of the owner of the office building, "a radiant, magnificent young creature, splendid, like all her mates, with the new and eager splendor of a long-awaited opportunity," appears, at an opera performance, only at the end of the book. A newly married husband in the audience has never seen her before, but "he knew that she was Cecilia Ingles, and his heart was constricted at the sight of her. It is for such a woman that one man builds a Clifton and that a hundred others are martyred in it."

*The Cliff-Dwellers*, which takes for its subject the accidental modern unit of the office building, the diversity of human beings who have it in common that they are thrown together by working there, was perhaps suggested by Zola, and it anticipates such similar books as Waldo Frank's *City Block* and Dos Passos's *Manhattan Transfer*. *With the Procession*, a better novel, is closer to the tradition of Howells—the low-keyed, prosaic domestic chronicle. But, having done his duty by Chicago in these studies of a social organism, the author, still involved with his city, went on to pieces of lesser scope, in which he is more himself and more enjoyable today than in either of these solider novels or in his fantasies of leisured Europeans.

Fuller said that he hated Chicago and that if it were not for his family interests he would leave it and go to live in Italy, and he advised Hamlin Garland, a young writer from Wisconsin, since Garland did not have to stay there, to leave. But he was not entirely unmoved by the cultural ambitions of the city, which was ridiculed in the East for some Chicagoan's statement that Chicago was going to "make culture hum." Chicago was to have its Art Institute and its Opera, both genuinely superior institutions. An excellent literary review, the *Dial,* to which

Fuller often contributed, had been started in Chicago in 1880 and was to remain there till 1916; the *Chap-Book,* in the *Yellow Book* tradition, which ran from 1894 to 1898, published Yeats and Henry James; and *Poetry,* which printed the early work of Eliot, Pound, and other then unknown but later famous poets and to which Fuller acted as adviser, was started in 1912. In 1890, the University of Chicago had been founded, with Rockefeller money. Its first president, William R. Harper, of Ohio, a leading Hebrew scholar who had been teaching at Yale, was a man full of enthusiasm and innovating ideas, and he brought to the West an extraordinary faculty, which included, on the side of the humanities (the scientific side was equally remarkable): in English—Robert M. Lovett of Massachusetts and Harvard; William Vaughn Moody, the poet and dramatist, of Indiana and Harvard; Robert Herrick, the novelist, of Cambridge and Harvard; and John M. Manly, the Chaucerian scholar, of Alabama and Harvard; in Classics—Paul Shorey of Iowa and Harvard; and in History—Ferdinand Schevill of Ohio and Yale, and the Baltic outlaw H. E. von Holst, who became an authority on American history. Thorstein Veblen spent fourteen years and wrote *The Theory of the Leisure Class* at Chicago, and John Dewey was at one time director of the school of education. This group of scholars and writers combined the best of the East with the best of the Middle West who had been educated in the East. Some of them had studied in Europe, and many spent their vacations there. They equaled, if they did not surpass, the group that Woodrow Wilson not much later (1902) was able to recruit for Princeton. I have heard Robert Lovett tell of the high missionary spirit with which these young men set out to create from scratch, in what had lately been a swampy waste, a great emporium of learning and inspiration. Robert Herrick, so thorough a New Eng-

lander, fastidious and rather thin-skinned, was to remain
in Chicago thirty years, and in his entertaining novel
*Chimes,* though putting on record the crudity and disorder of the university's early days and its struggles with
its backers and trustees, he brings out the bold aims of the
president and the courage and goodwill of the pioneering
teachers. The university did provide an intellectual center
for the competitive scramble that Fuller described, and he
followed its activities with much interest, as he did the
artistic activities of the city. He established close relations
with the academic people, and he responded with lively
interest to any manifestations of talent on the part of
young painters or writers. His spirit seems to have been
pervasive, and the tributes collected after his death by
Anna Morgan, the manager of a little theater, are evidence of the gratitude of his colleagues, who felt the
stimulus of the presence among them of a craftsman of
very high standards who had put himself to school to the
finest of the scholarship and art of the world. And the
novelist, on his side, diverted himself by writing about
these cultural exploits.

In 1901, Fuller published a group of three stories called
*Under the Skylights.* Perhaps the best of these, "The
Downfall of Abner Joyce," is based on the career of Hamlin Garland. Abner Joyce, on coming to Chicago, writes
stark and indignant stories about the rigors of life on the
Western farms and affects to despise the activities of what
he regards as an effete intelligentsia, but when he finds
himself taken up by them and given an entrée into the
social life of Chicago he develops an appetite for it and is
obviously very much gratified at becoming a fashionable
figure. This characterization is amply confirmed by the
four volumes of Garland's memoirs, in which he recounts
at length his relations with many celebrities of the literary
and political and moreyed worlds, whom he never missed

a chance of seeing and whose kindness to and praise of
himself he obviously loved to chronicle. He was always
presiding at meetings of academies and getting up artists'
clubs. When he organized such a club in Chicago and
called it the Cliff-Dwellers, after Fuller's novel, Fuller—
no doubt embarrassed—refused to become a member, or
even, Garland says, so far as he knows, to accept an invita-
tion to dine there. Yet it is evidence of Fuller's generosity
where anyone of real talent was concerned that, in spite of
his portrait of Garland as something of a bumpkinish
climber, he should have remained on good terms with him
all his life and that he did not forfeit Garland's respect.
He was evidently, however, to return to the subject in
another little comedy, called "Addolorata's Intervention."
Here the character who represents Fuller and the character who represents Garland accidentally meet in Sicily.
The former, a novelist who has never had much audience,
cannot but feel that the latter, now a popular writer, is
treating him with a cavalier condescension. He meets,
also, a young lady fan of his own unpopular works, but
he praises his rival to her, and she immediately attaches
herself to the other, who eagerly snatches her up. The
first writer, who is conscious of his superiority and really
does not care about the girl, looks on at the whole comedy
with a detachment not untinged by a certain disdainful
envy.

It should be said at this point, in parenthesis, before we
pass in review the more successful books of Fuller, that he
was curiously unsuccessful and gave evidence of unexpectedly uncertain taste when he tried to work in any
other form or vein than those of his ironic fiction. *The
Puppet-Booth* (1896), which followed *With the Procession,* is a collection of little plays—with Maeterlinck
somewhere in the background—that depart from the realistic without managing to achieve the poetic. And when

the *Spoon River Anthology* of Edgar Lee Masters appeared in 1915, Fuller was excited by it and thought that this kind of epitaph in vers libre or broken prose had interesting possibilities. Two years later, he published a book of such epitaphs called *Lines Long and Short*, but they lack the grim pathos of Masters. Fuller here is simply sketching the same kind of characters that appear in his novels, but with much less telling effect. In the meantime, in 1899, he had been provoked by the war with Spain and our occupation of the Philippines to a quite uncharacteristic outbreak—a satire in verse called *The New Flag*. He was unable to find a publisher for what was thought, in that imperialistic era, an antipatriotic tirade and had it printed at his own expense. *The New Flag* is ill-written as verse and even rather coarse in its violence. Robert Lovett, in an article in *The New Republic* at the time of Fuller's death, expressed the opinion that this blast had a bad effect on Fuller's career: it made him unpopular in Chicago, and what was worse, it deranged and poisoned a temperament and a talent which were normally calm and aloof. McKinley's invasion of the Philippines, with its two years of war on the natives, was an act of gratuitous conquest that shocked men who had forgotten the Mexican War and accepted the Civil War— men such as Mark Twain and William Vaughn Moody, who protested with blistering bitterness. It is significant that the part-time expatriate Fuller, who ridiculed and deplored the tendencies of contemporary America, should still have retained enough of old-fashioned American idealism to flare up and give vent to such vituperation.

*Under the Skylights* was followed, in 1908, by *Waldo Trench and Others: Stories of Americans in Italy*, which exploits much more successfully the same materials as an earlier collection, of 1898, *From the Other Side: Stories of Transatlantic Travel*. The European figures of these earlier stories are the phantoms of a consolatory daydream, but the Americans abroad of *Waldo Trench* represent situations at home of which Fuller had had firsthand experience. In the story which gives the volume its title, a young man from Oklahoma is first seen much moved and excited at discovering, in downtown New York, a church which is 150 years old. "How it brings back the old Revolutionary days!" he exclaims. "I expect to see few things more impressive than this." But he is on his way to Europe, and when he gets there he discovers the Renaissance, by which he is even more excited. He is infatuated with Van Dyck and Raphael, Brunelleschi and Isabella d'Este, till someone puts him on to the Middle Ages, and he decides that Isabella d'Este is inferior to Dante's Beatrice and that he must go at once to Assisi. But then he is told by someone that classical Rome is the thing if one wants "to get the foundations of a good solid education," and while he is doing Rome, someone else tells him that "the Etruscans were the first schoolmasters of the Romans. They whipped those poor, uncouth creatures into shape and passed them on to the Greeks," so Trench goes to study the Etruscan cities. But poking among their ruins, he runs into an Englishman who exclaims to him scornfully, "Why, they're only Etruscan!" "What did you expect them to be?" " 'I'm after the Pelasgians,' [the Englishman] returned in the sourest tone imaginable; 'what is this modern world to *me?*' " The next step back into the European past would be to explore the remains of the early Sicilian rock-dwellers, "called Sikelians or Sicanians." But a friend, with mischievous intent, explains at once to Waldo that these names belong to two different groups: "The distinction between them is an important one and well worthy of the best endeavors of an ambitious young *savant.*" In the meantime, he has met a rich girl from Ohio, whose aunt, also rich, is pulsing with the spirit of Western enterprise and discourages Waldo's researches. She thinks that he is headed in the wrong direction: "That young man," she declares. "Such amazing vigor, such exhaustless driving power, such astonishing singleness of purpose! And all, at present, so misapplied. Think what such qualities are going to effect for him on those farms and in the civic life of his new commonwealth!" He gives up his ambition to penetrate the past, and marries the niece and returns to Oklahoma.

Another of these stories, "For the Faith," seems to me a comic masterpiece. It presents in a few pages a whole cultural shift in American life and might well be included in the reading list of a course in American history. A young schoolteacher from Stoneham Falls, Connecticut, is taking, with a couple of other girls, a vacation trip to Europe and writing to a friend at home. She finds herself on the boat with a very well-known "plutocrat," to whom she always refers with a proper New Enggland scorn both snobbish and moralistic. But the plutocrat has with him an agreeable nephew, who pays the young lady compliments and seems to feel a real interest in her. She, however, maintains her attitude and, when she meets them again on her travels, insists to him that he and his uncle only want to buy up European art treasures and take them back to America: "Oh, leave those poor things alone! Let the land that originated them keep them a little longer. They were born here and they belong here. Restrain yourself. I'd much rather you went back to America and learned to rob your fellow-citizens." But Philippa, as in those days they used to say, has set her cap for young Thorpe. She has at first been writing of her plans for doing England in the usual guidebook way—"Salisbury and Winchester and Wells" —but she afterward manages an itinerary which enables her to keep up her acquaintance with the plutocrat and his nephew. Eventually, she bags her prey. The young man, when he gets back to the States, is going to have a job in one of his uncle's companies in Colorado, and she looks forward to being founder and president of the first women's club in the town. The modulation from her original point of view into complete acceptance of the millionaire is accomplished by Fuller with much humorous subtlety. Though her tone remains equally priggish, she now has a rationalization for her approval of everything she condemned before: "We cannot have an omelet without breaking a few eggs; we cannot bring a vast new country under the plough without turning under, at the same time, a certain number of innocent flowers; nor can a man seat himself at the apex of an enormous fortune without the charge of many minor injustices from a chorus of outspoken enemies. The old gentleman—whom I at last view not as a sociological abstraction but as a human creature like the rest of us—has probably had his beliefs and convictions, after all, and has in some degree suffered and sacrificed himself for them." What puts everything on a perfectly sound basis is discovering that the millionaire was, like herself, a product of the Naugatuck Valley: "He had been born on a farm *near* Stoneham Falls and been carried over into Fairfield County at the age of one."

Fuller published in the *Dial* in 1917 "A Plea for Shorter Novels," which is based, among other considerations, on the needlessness of writing descriptions of such places as everyone knows and of characters whom the reader will in any case identify with people he has seen. He "would sweep away . . . all laborious effort on stuff that is dragged in because someone will think it 'ought to be there'—clichés, conventional scenes and situations." In the next year, he published *On the Stairs,* which seems to me one of his best things. I used to amuse myself by telling foreign visitors that it was "the great American novel."

(I find that James Huneker, in a letter to Fuller, calls it "the great Chicago novel.") *On the Stairs* deals with life in Chicago, but it dispenses with realistic trappings, and the author explains in a foreword that the book is an attempt at the kind of thing which he has recently been recommending. His device in this story is to tell it much as if he were an old Chicagoan recounting to another Chicagoan who takes the town and the milieu for granted the inside story of families that both of them have known. In the last quarter of the last century, two boys grow up in the city. One of them, Raymond Prince, is the son of a well-to-do family, who, like Fuller's, has come to the West, by way of New York State, from New England; the other, Johnny McComas, is the son of their stableman, who has lived with his family in the stable. Raymond breaks away, like Fuller, from the family background of banking and real estate, studies architecture and art, and spends a few years in Europe. In the meantime, Johnny has left school early, has worked hard, and soon becomes envied and admired as "the youngest bank-president in the 'Loop.'" We follow thereafter the progress of Johnny, as he grows more and more prosperous, and the gradual subsidence of Raymond, who has no interest in the family bank—it eventually goes into receivership—but never succeeds in doing anything of any worth in line with his artistic tastes. Raymond's discontented wife from the East, to his bitter humiliation, divorces him and marries Johnny, and Raymond is now so impoverished that he is obliged to let Johnny put his son through Yale. To make matters even worse from the point of view of Raymond, this son marries Johnny's daughter, a daughter by an earlier, very bourgeois wife. Now, in a story by Henry James, it would be made clear that Raymond had the finer values and that his frustration was not without nobility; in a story by Horatio Alger, Johnny would be a self-made hero who had achieved the kind of success that every American wants. But the point of Fuller's novel is that the two men are equally mediocre and that the social distinctions which originally divided them have in two generations disappeared. Raymond, to be sure, is pathetic, but we do not much sympathize with him. Johnny is relatively impressive by reason of his masculine vigor, and he behaves in a not ungenerous way, but he remains rather coarse and discomforting, and we do not like *him* much, either. Huneker compared *On the Stairs* to Flaubert's *Bouvard et Pécuchet*.

The futility of the young man who comes back to Chicago from Europe with greater sophistication and polish but enfeebled qualifications for making himself a place in the world of his origin has already been illustrated by Fuller in Truesdale Marshall of *With the Procession*. This is, in fact, with Fuller a recurrent theme—a kind of caricature of one aspect of himself. But he was not, of course, himself an ineffectual dilettante. Continuing to live in his native city and, as he once told Garland, with "no expectation of seeing satisfactory improvement in this town during my lifetime," he remained nevertheless indefatigable in his attempts to encourage anyone who showed any sign of serious cultural ambition. He put himself at the service of young painters and writers; with the latter, he read and criticized their manuscripts and even corrected their proofs. For years he conducted a book department in one of the daily papers. The volume of "Tributes to Henry B. from friends in whose minds and hearts he will always live" (the title on the cover is *Henry B. Fuller*), compiled by Anna Morgan, shows how many and what various people felt that they owed him a debt: Jane Addams, Louis Bromfield, Hamlin Garland, Lorado Taft, the sculptor; Bert Leston Taylor, the columnist; John T. McCutcheon, the cartoonist and illustra-

tor; Harriet Monroe, the editor of *Poetry;* Thornton
Wilder, Booth Tarkington, and other figures less well
known. A good many of them seemed to feel that, less
successful than some of them, he was somehow a little
above them. At every gathering he was eagerly expected,
though he did not always appear. Like many intelligent
and affectionate born bachelors, he counted very much
on his friends. He looked on sympathetically at their family relations and liked to amuse their children, with whom
he was very popular and to whom he sometimes stood
godfather; he would make the evenings gay by playing
and enjoying old songs. But about his own life he was
always guarded. He was supposed to have a room in his
mother's house, but actually he seemed to live, says his
biographer, Constance M. Griffin, "in a succession of
rooming houses, where he could not be reached by telephone, and where no one would presume to call." No one
ever knew his address, and he was regarded as something
of a "mystery." This way of life is partly to be explained
by his dislike of being disturbed, his scrupulous inde-
pendence, and his resolute intention, so unaccountable
in Chicago, not to have to make any money beyond his
modest family income. In a society in which, as Fuller
describes it, one's status depended on one's income and
in which, as a consequence, this status was always precarious, he chose to maintain the cultural prestige to
which he had been born in the city by accepting somewhat sordid conditions of living. Hamlin Garland complains of Fuller that he has "lived so long in restaurants
that his table manners annoy me. He automatically pol-
ishes his coffee cup and wipes all the forks and knives on
his napkin or on a corner of the tablecloth. He turns each
piece of toast (looking for a possible fly) and peers into
the milk or cream jug for a cockroach, all of which is
funny for a time but comes to be an irritation at last—

and yet he is the ablest, most distinctive, most intellectual of all our Western writers. He can be—and generally is— the most satisfactory of all my literary companions." Though Garland says in his memoirs that he was irked by Fuller's faultfinding, the adjective most often applied to him in the Morgan collection of tributes is "gentle." It is said of him that though his character was essentially steely, his manner in company was shy. Burton Rascoe thus described him in a "profile" of 1924: "In person Mr. Fuller is a furtive little fellow with a neatly trimmed white beard and white hair; his skin is smooth and white; his voice is soft and hesitant; his eyes gleam with amused inquisitiveness; and he is always perfectly shod and tailored. He is neat, gracious, charming, excessively quiet." In the photographs of Fuller in his later years, one notes always a slight look of anxiety.

There was perhaps another reason for the secrecy of Fuller's habits. He was evidently homosexual. This seems obvious throughout his work, in which he prefers to dwell on the splendid physiques of his young male characters rather than on the attractions of the women. He has a tendency, as in *On the Stairs*, to favor his vigorous vulgarians at the expense of his effete *raffinés*. On the death of Rudolph Valentino, Fuller wrote, but did not publish, a eulogy of this "Sheik" of the movies, who was apparently, according to Mencken's account of his curious interview with him, a genuinely sensitive fellow. Though certain conventionally desirable matings do occur in Fuller's novels, the situations that involve the affections are likely to be those in which some older man—it was apparently Fuller's problem—is trying to find a sympathetic younger man to live or travel with him. In his "Plea for Shorter Novels," he includes among elements to be eliminated "reluctant love passages" and "repellent sex discussions." But this emphasis was undoubtedly one of the reasons—together with his resolve to avoid "scenes of violence and bloodshed with which one may have no proper affinity" and "indelicate 'close-ups' which explore and exploit poor humanity beyond the just bounds of decorum"—for Fuller's lack of popularity. The novelists of that sentimental period—Owen Wister in *The Virginian* and George Cable in *The Cavalier*—were capable of glorifying virility in a way that probably flushed with pride their masculine readers as well as excited their large feminine audience, but Fuller was incapable of such specious romance: he is ironic about even his handsome young men. His books contain no sex interest of any kind. It is all the more startling, then, that he should suddenly, in *The Puppet-Booth*—in one of his short plays, called *At Saint Judas's*—have given such frank expression to that element of his personality. This rather absurd piece— Fuller is bad when he tries to be overtly dramatic—is concerned with the crisis that precedes a wedding, when the best man, the bridegroom's close friend, with whom he has been sharing rooms, turns up in the sacristy of the church in a state of hysterical emotion and tells the groom that he must not get married, that the prospective bride is a slut, that she has been going to bed with him, the best man. In this story, however, he soon breaks down, knowing well that the other will not believe it: "I am here. And *she* will never be. You may wait, but you shall wait in vain. (*He places his hand upon the other's shoulder.*) If she were to come, I should not let her have you. She shall not have you. Nobody shall have you." A horrible scene ensues—a scene too horrible for Fuller to handle. The friend attempts to bar the groom from entering the church. The groom says, "Stand aside. I hate you; I detest you; I despise you; I loathe you." "We have been friends always," the other replies. "I have loved you all my life. . . . The thought of *her* made me mad, made me desperate." He declares that one of the three shall die. The bridegroom invites him to "use your blade" (he evidently refers to a sword). The bride is coming up the aisle, and the groom enters the church. *"Upon the floor of the sacristy lies the body of a man in a pool of blood."* The trouble here is that Fuller is incapable of imagining at all convincingly such an outbreak of naked passion—especially between characters who are carrying swords. I agree with Miss Griffin when she says that the middle-aged Freiherr von Kaltenau, as he appears in *The Last Refuge,* traveling with an adored young man, is to be identified with Fuller when this character, taking stock of his life, concludes that it "had been indeed too free—too free from ties, from duties, from obligations, from restraints; too free from guidance, too free from the kindly pressure of any ordering hand. . . . The book of life had been opened wide before him, but he had declined to make the usual advance that leads straight on from chapter to chapter; rather had he fluttered the leaves carelessly, glanced at the end before reaching the middle, and thoroughly thwarted the aims and intentions of the great Author." I agree that the author identifies himself also with another of the people in this book, a novelist whose "principal concern was the portrayal of his contemporaries in works of fiction," when he confesses that his "participation in life has been, after all, but partial. I have always felt a slight reluctance about committing myself—a touch of dread about letting myself go. I have lived, in fact, by the seashore without ever venturing into the water. Others have gone in before my eyes, and I have recorded, to the best of my endeavor, the exhilarations they appeared to feel, the dangers they appeared to brave. But as soon as the waves have stolen up to my own toes, I have always stepped back upon the dry sands."

"There was in its deepest recesses," writes Harriet Monroe of Fuller's character, without assigning a specific cause, "an unconquerable reticence—Henry Fuller found it impossible to tell his whole story. He could not give himself away, and therefore it may be that the greatest book of which his genius was capable was never written, the book which would have brought the world to his feet in complete accord and delight." But one cannot imagine Fuller's writing such a book, and when he did reveal his secret, so far from bringing the world to his feet, he made it look the other way. In 1919, when he was sixty-two, he took the audacious step of publishing a novel, *Bertram Cope's Year,* with homosexual characters. His attitude about this at first is quite unabashed and cool: "I wrote," he tells Henry Kitchell Webster, another Illinois novelist, "in complete reaction from the love flummery of Holworthy Hall, et al. [Holworthy Hall was a pseudonym, the name of one of the Harvard dormitories, used by Harold Everett Porter, a writer for *Collier's* and *The Saturday Evening Post.*] Those fellows tire me. Perhaps I've gone too far the other way. While doing the job, I *did* think, now and then, of some of your own aberrations and perversions (Olga, Helena, et cet.)—but these in latter-day society are getting almost too common to be termed 'abnormal.' Lots of people must have read you in unperturbed innocency, and I hope a good many will read me that way, too. Certainly we are both 'Innocent Kids' compared with Cabell in *Jurgen.*" And *Bertram Cope's Year,* though it involves homosexual situations, is not really a book about homosexuality. It has a kind of philosophic theme, which seems to me to raise it well above the fiction of social surfaces of the school of William Dean Howells. The story is made to take place in a Middle Western university town, which derives, Fuller admits, to some extent from Evanston, Illinois. Bertram Cope is a young instructor who is working for an M.A. in English. He is very good-looking, with yellow hair, and not stupid, though not strikingly intelligent, and he is found attractive by a number of persons. There is, first, Mr. Basil Randolph, a "scholar *manqué*," who works in the family brokerage business but is far more interested in collecting jades and other *objets d'art* and in hovering around the male students, who are likely themselves to be hovering around the quadrangle that houses the girls. There is also Medora Phillips, a well-to-do widow, who likes to have young people around her and has living in the house with her a niece, a girl secretary, and a girl boarder. All these people become infatuated with Bertram, who does not become attached to any of them. He is said to be "an ebullient Puritan," with New England perhaps in the background, and he is interested only in making his way. The niece traps him into an engagement, from which he afterward manages to extricate himself; the more aggressive boarder, who is fearfully jealous of the niece, tries to ensnare him by painting his portrait; the secretary writes him sonnets which are considered by the older generation to go pretty far for a young girl. And Mrs. Phillips herself—though he regards her merely as a person to whose house he is glad to go—becomes much preoccupied with Bertram. The designs of Mr. Randolph are frustrated—he has taken new rooms, with an extra bedroom—when Bertram himself takes new rooms in order to accommodate a friend with whom he has been intimately corresponding and whom he brings on to keep him company. This friend, whose name is Arthur Lemoyne, Mr. Randolph does not at first want to meet and, when he does, immediately recognizes as the wrong kind of homosexual and resents as a dangerous rival: "His dark eyes were too liquid; his person was too plump," etc. Lemoyne, on his side, has brought pressure on Bertram to get out of his engagement with the niece, and he now pits himself against Randolph and all the ladies of the Phillips household. But nothing can dispel the enchantment which Bertram continues to exercise over all of them. When he tips over in a small sailboat, he is saved by his fiancée, who disentangles him from the mainsail and cordage, but he gets credit for having saved *her;* when the Phillips cottage on the dunes is broken into by an escaped convict, Bertram merely wakes up with a shriek while another man grapples with the burglar, but it is Bertram who becomes the hero. When he passes out at a dinner as the result of drinking wine, to which he is not accustomed, on top of a day of excessive work and a more or less empty stomach, he becomes the object of everyone's attention and everyone's solicitude. Mrs. Phillips's rather sour brother-in-law, crippled and half-blind, who plays the role of the detached observer and is completely aware of what is going on, growls that it all reminds him of a religious festival he once attended in an Italian hill town near Florence: "There was a kind of grotto in the church, under the high altar; and in the grotto was a full-sized figure of a dead man, carved and painted—and covered with wounds; and round that figure half the women and girls of the town were collected, stroking, kissing . . . Adonis all over again!"

This establishes the real point of the story, which is that Bertram's admirers all look to find in him a version of a semidivine ideal that he makes no attempt to live up to; that he is quite unconscious that his beauty and charm, together with a hard, self-sufficient core of character, have caused them to endow him with qualities which he does not at all possess. In the end, he simply gets his degree and leaves. But in the meantime he has been separated from Arthur Lemoyne. The latter has taken a feminine role in a college musical comedy and has had a unique success as a female impersonator; after the play, he has disgraced himself behind the scenes by making advances to a boy who has been playing a male part. His connection with the college is tenuous—something arranged by Bertram, through Randolph—and the authorities let him go. Bertram appeals to Randolph, who refuses to be helpful, and Arthur, with his bad reputation, is now a nuisance, anyhow, to Bertram. Bertram goes East and gets a better job in a better university. Randolph and Mrs. Phillips talk about him after he has left. She believes that when Bertram is earning enough, he will marry her secretary, the only one of his friends to whom he has written, though in a quite noncommittal way; Randolph, on the contrary, believes that Bertram will set up housekeeping with Arthur. At no point has the reader been given any clue as to Bertram's sexual inclinations. Fuller's rather difficult problem here has been to make Bertram intrinsically uninteresting and even rather comic, but at the same time to dramatize convincingly the spell of enchantment he is supposed to cast. This is seen in his effect on the other characters, but the reader is not made to feel it: Bertram is represented as behaving in an agreeable enough way, but in his self-centeredness, he never does anything that is made to seem really attractive. And the result, as in *On the Stairs*, is a kind of deliberate flatness.

This curious book, which is perhaps Fuller's best, seems never to have had adequate attention. The few people who have written about Fuller at any length have, so far as my reading goes, always treated it very gingerly. The only contemporary, so far as I know, who showed any real appreciation was James Huneker, who very much prided himself on his sophistication and lack of prudery and had previously applauded *At Saint Judas's*. He wrote Fuller of *Bertram Cope's Year* that he had read it three times: "Its portraiture and psychological strokes fill me with envy and also joy. *Ça y est,* I said to myself. And Chicago! It is as desolate, your dissection, as a lunar landscape. We are like that, not like Whitman's Camerados and his joyful junk. Why do you speak of your last book! You are only beginning, you implacable Stendhal of the lake!" But otherwise the effect of the novel was a slighting reproof or a horrified silence. André Gide had then only the prestige of a very limited cult; Proust had not yet been translated. Burton Rascoe wrote, "It may be said that *Bertram Cope's Year,* in so far as it was read and understood at all, shocked Mr. Fuller's friends so painfully that they silenced it into limbo. It is a story, delicately done with the most exquisite taste, of a sublimated irregular affection. It received scant and unintelligent notice from the reviewers, and though it was filled with dynamite scrupulously packed, it fell as harmless as a dud, only to be whispered about here and there by grave people who wondered why Mr. Fuller should choose such a theme." But even this writer of the early twenties who wants to do justice to Fuller does not accurately describe the book. The central theme, as I have said above, is not "a sublimated irregular affection." Fuller has merely, in writing of the power exerted by a "charismic" personality, extended what was then the conventional range. The effect on poor Fuller himself of the reception of his book was terrible. He disparaged his own courage by saying that he wished he had never written it, and he burned up his manuscript and proofs. It was ten years before he ventured to publish another novel.

He returned in 1929, in *Gardens of This World*—of which I have already spoken—to his beloved group of Old World characters. "Such a goddam lovely little book," he says in a letter to one of his young friends. *Not on the Screen,* which was published in 1930, is the last of his Chicago novels and not only the most stripped but the palest of them; yet Fuller is always readable and always winning, through his dry sense of comedy. The book begins with a movie which a girl and a young man are watching. In the picture, there is a melodramatic situation. The rest of the novel is the story of the subsequent relations of the couple, which repeats the story of the film but is not at all melodramatic. The upstart young man from the country wins the hand of the rich young girl without any very stiff struggle. There are some rather disagreeable but not very dramatic encounters between this modest but successful young man and a socially well-situated and insolent young banker who is competing for the hand of the girl. The banker, who has power of attorney for the girl's widowed mother, resorts to unscrupulous practices in his efforts to gain his end, by threatening to ruin the family and attempting to send the young man to jail. But, although in the film the corresponding character is made to play the role of the villain, the character in the novel is not himself sent to jail. He is never melodramatically unmasked, but, in a quiet way, pressure is put upon him to restore the family fortunes. The mistress of the young banker, who would figure as the "vamp" in the picture, is a cheap and rather pathetic figure who, although she arouses suspicion by going out with the *jeune premier*, has never for a moment tempted him. The story is all told in terms of the social nuances of Chicago, of which Fuller was an amused observer, but the point of the whole thing is that in a Western city like Chicago—and perhaps, by implication, anywhere in the United States—these differences matter very little. You cannot get a thrilling drama out of them. This novel is another exercise in the art of making it flat—the quality of which art, of course, was appreciated little by the public and which accounts for the lessening interest in the books of Fuller's later years.

In this very late last burst of energy—Fuller was now seventy-two—he started still another novel, but he did not get far with this or see the publication of either *Not on the Screen* or *Gardens of This World*. He died alone in a rooming house in July 1929. One is reminded of the ending of one of the character sketches in *Lines Long and Short*, the portrait of a familyless bachelor who has tried to make a life for himself by his attentions to the families of friends and who is left with little consolation:

> Yes, perhaps he did
> Come through all right—
> With much or little sympathy—
> To take up, with what zest he could,
> The frantic role
> Of buying favors from a cooling world.
> Spend as you will,
> It's sad to be old, and alone.
> (Fudge! that's the very thing
> I tried hard not to say!)

The literature on Fuller is extremely meager. Besides the volume of tributes mentioned and a few other scattered memoirs, there is only the inadequate biography by Constance M. Griffin—evidently one of those theses which the estimable Arthur H. Quinn of the University of Pennsylvania, the author of comprehensive and useful books on American fiction and drama, induced his students to write on neglected American authors. We must be grateful to Mr. Quinn. If it had not been for him, we should have had nothing of value at all on such writers as Kate Chopin and Fuller. But something more searching and solid is needed, and now that the University of Chicago Press has reprinted *With the Procession,* I should like to suggest that it commission a life and letters of Fuller, as well as a volume of his uncollected pieces. He did a good deal of reviewing in his lifetime. I have just been through the articles he contributed to *The New Republic* during the twenties when he was not writing novels. They are always discriminating and conscientious, and it is interesting to know what he thought about Chekhov, Cabell, and Proust. Miss Griffin's selective bibliography includes many other items which awaken curiosity, as well as a long list of unpublished or uncollected stories. We know from those stories of Kate Chopin and Cable which were rejected by the conventional magazines of the nineties and the early 1900's that some of these authors' most interesting things were inacceptable to the squeamish editors. Fuller's early humorous writings for *Life* should also be investigated. I have looked up "A Transcontinental Episode, or, Metamorphoses at Muggins' Misery: A Co-operative Novel by Bret James and Henry Harte" (published in 1884). It is juvenile but not unamusing. A Jamesian young man who has lived abroad and is always slipping into French arrives in one of Harte's tough California settlements. He falls in love with the local belle and she with him, as the result of which he tries to transform himself into the kind of man he thinks she admires. But she, on her side, during an absence of his, has schooled herself to be refined. Fuller supplies two alternative endings, by each of the collaborators. In Harte's version, when her lover returns in the garb of a rugged Westerner, she casts off her elegant clothes and with a whoop leaps into his arms. In James's, she preserves the "finer" manners and dress to which her contact with the traveled young Easterner has raised her, but the question of whether they can ever now get together is left, in the Jamesian fashion, completely up in the air. This little skit foreshadows the theme of the constant conflict between the two states of American culture which was to occupy Fuller all his life.

May 23, 1970

# TWO NEGLECTED AMERICAN NOVELISTS

## II. Harold Frederic, the Expanding Upstater

Henry B. Fuller and Harold Frederic may be appropriately treated together because each had intensively studied, in the last decades of the nineteenth century, a certain section of American society—Fuller Chicago, Frederic upstate New York—and both had used the local background for ambitious and distinguished fiction of a kind encouraged by the fatherly example of William Dean Howells. They are likely to be ticked off rather briefly in the academic histories of American literature in a chapter with some such title as "The Beginnings of American Realism." But these two highly individual writers ought not thus to be reduced to so dreary a classification. Each deserves a serious attention such as Fuller has never been given and Frederic is only now beginning to get.

A first attempt to deal adequately with Frederic was made by Thomas F. O'Donnell and Hoyt C. Franchere in a small volume, published in 1961, of the undiscriminating and often inept Twayne series, but the dimensions of the series itself, together with the double authorship, prevented this—though Mr. O'Donnell, of Utica College, who was born in Frederic's country, is one of the best-equipped authorities on him—from becoming the full-length study that Harold Frederic deserves. An important critical contribution has now, however, been made by *The Novels of Harold Frederic,* by Austin Briggs, Jr., of Hamilton College (also in Frederic's country). This book represents at its best the work of intelligent scholarship in the field of American literature. Mr. Briggs has rescued Frederic from the category of bitter realist to which previous academic critics have too cursorily consigned him, and has analyzed his books from the points of view of Frederic's favorite themes and the general ideas conveyed, which go far beyond mere local realism. The fat footnotes are not the usual unnecessary padding, laid down as a stratum at the bottom of the pages to meet the requirements demanded of an academic job, but contain a good deal that is interesting. The book places Harold Frederic firmly, with all his intellectual range, on the American and international literary map. (Other sources on which I have been able to draw are the papers on Frederic by Stanton Garner, of Brown University, and the unpublished dissertation by Paul Haines, of Auburn University, the last especially valuable for its biographical information.)

Mr. Briggs has brought out Frederic's character in a way that makes him a striking contrast with Fuller. Henry Fuller was a thorough New Englander of the later, less vigorous breed, who remained uncoarsened by early Chicago. His family were well-to-do, and Fuller had enjoyed "advantages." He had early got away to Europe and, as a traveler never much involved in the affairs of the foreign countries he visited, had acquired detailed knowledge of their history and their arts. He was fastidious and somewhat shrinking. Harold Frederic had nothing of New England: he came of Dutch and German stock—the name was originally Fredericksz—which, in America, had never been out of New York State. His ancestors had been eight generations of pioneer farmers and craftsmen in the Hudson and Mohawk Valleys. His father had modestly prospered as a finisher of chairs in Utica, but his health was impaired by the confinement and by breathing the fumes of shellac that this kind of work imposed, and he was finally obliged to give it up and take a job as freight conductor on the New York Central Railroad. He was killed when his train ran off the track and the cars were plunged down an embankment. Harold was then scarcely two. His mother now made a living as a seamstress. He graduated from school at fifteen and immediately began working as a printer and photographer's assistant. At nineteen, he joined the staff of the Utica *Observer,* and at twenty-four became its editor. It is evidence of the excellence in that period of the local education and libraries that he had learned at an early age to write lucidly and with precision. He went on, two years later, to the editorship of the Albany *Evening Journal.* He was, in consequence, deeply involved in the politics of New York State. Though he worked on a Republican paper, he had always admired Horatio Seymour, the Democratic governor, and eventually became a journalist for the Democrats; he later contributed his influence to electing Grover Cleveland governor. In 1884, when Frederic was twenty-eight, he was sent to London by *The New York Times* as its regular correspondent, and he not only covered the British news but visited and reported on Ireland and published series of articles on the cholera epidemic in France, the young German Emperor Wilhelm II, and the persecution of the Jews in Russia. He was gregarious, liked London club life, and was a rather aggressive conversationalist. Fuller, although his work is quite distinct from James's, belongs to Henry James's world, but Frederic, according to Thomas Beer, declared that Henry

James was "an effeminate old donkey who lives with a
herd of other donkeys around him and insists on being
treated as if he were the Pope." An article signed simply
F., "by an Old Friend," which appeared in the *Saturday
Review* at the time of Frederic's death, says that Frederic
had "felt himself in Utica, in Albany, and in New York
very far above the men with whom he came into contact,
and thus he developed a habit of mind that did not always
ingratiate him with strangers. But he was capable when
he liked, and generally he did like, of exercising a wonderful charm over his intimates." He could dominate, this
writer continues, any company into which he came,
though he might make himself a bore in the same way
as Sinclair Lewis is said to have done in England by his
mimicries, when an "incident of perhaps somewhat re-
mote American life and manners, which happened to
interest him at the time, would be related in merciless
detail while the minutes passed into hours, and the reluctant audience thought of missed trains and neglected
appointments. But Frederic, the fury of the anecdotist
being upon him, would block the doorway with his towering bulk, and suffer no man to go till he had fashioned
the last link of the long chain, till he had elaborated his
theme with a Rabelaisian minuteness of detail." The polished and punctilious Conrad disliked Frederic and scornfully referred to him as "a journalist who had written
some novels."

Henry Fuller was a discreet homosexual and at the
same time something of a puritan. But the appetite of
Harold Frederic for attractive women was indomitable and
persistent. It appears in Frederic's work as well as in his
publicly irregular life. In his novels, he violates the genteel
conventions by allowing sex often to figure in its rawest,
least romantic form, though he makes an effort to veil it
from the more squeamish of his readers. In *Seth's Brother's*

*Wife,* the lady of the title goes so far as to fall little short of pulling her brother-in-law into bed, and it is discreetly made plain that the unfortunate Jessica of the title of *The Lawton Girl* has been at one time a prostitute. The first readers of *The Damnation of Theron Ware* must have shuddered at Theron's suspicion—which turns out, however, to be groundless—that Celia Madden is having an affair with the Catholic priest, Father Forbes. When W. T. Stead was publishing his exposé of London vice, which set off a persecution of prostitutes, Harold Frederic had the courage to defend them and to recommend replacing prostitution, as then practiced in London, with "affectionate and lasting concubinage" or "limited polyandry." And in London he himself performed the remarkable feat of simultaneously carrying on two households. He was already married to a girl from Utica, by whom he had had four children. A photograph shows her with short hair, vivacious, eager eyes which seem just on the verge of smiling, and eyebrows uptilted impishly. (Frederic himself had a blunt nose, thick lips, a bushy mustache of the period, and keenly practical yet potentially humorous eyes.) But a year after the last of her children was born, he met a young woman named Kate Lyon, also from upstate New York (Oswego), openly set up a household with her, and had by her three more children. His wife had not enjoyed, as did Harold, the social life of London —she seems to have had no woman friends—and he managed, with a minimum of scandal, to see such of his own friends as would meet his new mate and to take trips abroad with Kate Lyon. He continued, it is said, quite regularly to visit his other family.

In London, Harold Frederic began writing novels. These dealt at first with the world he had left behind, to which he still felt a lively loyalty and of which, as a newspaperman, he had absorbed a very thorough knowledge. He had already, before he came to Europe, begun, "after years of preparation," as he says, a novel about the Mohawk Valley at the time of the Revolution, but this was not finished till 1890, and before it was published Frederic had written two other novels on the life of this region as he had personally known it: *Seth's Brother's Wife,* which came out in 1887, and *The Lawton Girl,* which was published in the same year, 1890, as the first of these, *In the Valley.*

*In the Valley* has a certain interest for its picture of the hostile relations between the Dutch and the English colonists, and the strained situations that were peculiar at that time to New York, where a feudal tradition prevailed, as it did not do in New England, so that the farmers were driven to revolt, not so much against the king overseas as against the local Tory landowners. Harold Frederic makes this struggle come at last to a climax with the battle of Oriskany, near Utica, in which the aggrieved farmers confront and defeat the Tories, who had as allies the Mohawk Indians. But, as a story, *In the Valley* is wooden. It suffers from the stereotypes of its genre. The characters are all with such obvious design put through their historical paces that we never accept them as real individuals. Frederic later admitted that "their personalities always remained shadowy in my own mind."

Frederic's two other early novels display a more interesting talent. He did not here have to depend on study for his knowledge of nineteenth-century Utica and Albany. His powers of observation were remarkable, and as a journalist, he had had to train them. He was aware of all the social levels, the money interests, the political maneuverings that went to make the life of an upstate community. In *Seth's Brother's Wife* and *The Lawton Girl,* he presents almost every kind of person that was to be found at that time in such a city as Utica: the moderately well-to-do farmer; the swindler and the crooked politician; the newspaper editor who was venal and the honest one who was zealous for reform; the serious-minded schoolteacher; the family of rundown ex-canallers; the family who had in one generation been made rich by the "knitting mills" and who lived in a large square mansion and cultivated what I used to like to call—partly deriving, as I do, from that region—their cold-storage Utica gentility. The life in these farmlands and villages is not shown in a particularly cheerful light, and though the landscape is accurately described, its ennobling grandeur and splendor are hardly done justice by Frederic, who had almost no sense of poetry, who said frankly that he could not read it and that he had never written two lines of verse in his life. (It is noteworthy, also, that the poet Thomas H. Jones, Jr., living not far away, in Boonville, among some of the most beautiful scenery in the world, seems rarely, in his rather lush lyrics, to have written about his home surroundings but almost always about European landscapes.) You have, in these novels, the stultifying dullness of evenings on the old farm for a young man who has had to come back to it after working on a newspaper in the city; the embattled relations between workers and owners created by a lockout at the ironworks; the remorseless small-town machinations of confidence men and bankers. And Frederic very well conveys the nature of the life of a region which had only been settled at the end of the eighteenth century, where the communities had not wholly succeeded in finding their purpose and form. At one point in *The Lawton Girl,* one of the characters complains that all the able and ambitious people go away and never come back, while the mediocre stagnate at home, and in *Seth's Brother's Wife* a man who has abandoned the farm to become a successful New York City lawyer says that "Agriculture is out of date in this state.

Better let the old people live on their capital, as they go along. It's no use throwing good money after bad. Farm land here in the East is bound to decrease in value, steadily." In these novels, Harold Frederic has not yet been able entirely to free himself from the conventions of the fiction of the period. Though he always sticks conscientiously to real types and real conditions, he must not disappoint his readers by not having the stories come out right: the good man must get the good girl, morality must win in the end, and this is sometimes brought about in a way that is incongruous with the general tenor. On the other hand, as Frederic explains in the preface to the uniform edition of his fiction, he has found himself being distracted from his tendency to plan too methodically, in order to demonstrate something, by finding that "to my surprise at first, and then to my interested delight, the people [in *The Lawton Girl*] took matters into their own hands quite from the start. It seemed only by courtesy that I even presided over their meetings, and that my sanction was asked for their comings and goings." He now confesses that it had been "a false and cowardly thing" to kill off, in deference to the current proprieties, the once fallen Lawton girl, who has so nobly rehabilitated herself and who is pathetically made to protest on her deathbed, "I tell you I *have* lived it down!"

These novels were, beginning in 1893, to be followed by a series of short stories about New York State during the Civil War. The bibliography of these stories is somewhat confusing, for the longest, "The Copperhead," was published in America in a volume by itself and in England together with other stories, and the three collections published in America include different combinations. The whole sequence has now been collected by Mr. O'Donnell and brought out in a single volume, called *Harold Frederic's "Stories of York State."* In the preface to his uniform edition, the author says of these productions that "they are in large part my own recollections of the dreadful time—the actual things that a boy from five to nine saw or heard about him, while his own relatives were being killed, and his school-fellows orphaned, and women of his neighborhood forced into mourning and despair—and they had a right to be recorded." But remarkable though these stories are, it is surprising to find the author of *Theron Ware* declaring that they are "closer to my heart than any other work of mine, partly because they seem to me to contain the best things I have done or ever shall do, partly because they are so closely interwoven with the personal memories and experiences of my own childhood—and a little, also, no doubt, for the reason that they have not had the treatment outside that paternal affection has desired for them." Yet they are certainly, so far as I know, quite unlike any other fiction inspired by the Civil War, and in order to understand this difference we must look into the political background of the state of New York in the crisis.

New York during the Civil War was in the somewhat paradoxical position of supplying more soldiers for its population than any other state in the union and at the same time putting up in the East the strongest opposition to the Republican administration. The principal opponent of the policies of Lincoln was Governor Seymour, of Utica, who held office from 1853 to 1854 and from 1863 to 1864. Frederic, as has been said, was a great admirer of Seymour. This governor seems, in fact, to have been one of the chief influences in Frederic's early life. *In the Valley* was dedicated to his memory, and the example of Seymour's rectitude is said to have provided the compass by which Frederic steered himself, in his novels as well as in his journalism, through the complexities and the corruptions of New York State politics. His stories of the Civil

War period have the courage of a point of view which must have owed a good deal to Seymour. They reflect the peculiar mixture of patriotism and disaffection which was characteristic of their region and for which Seymour was so forthright a spokesman.

The role played by Seymour in respect to the war has been, from partisan bias, maliciously misrepresented. It soon became a part of the false mythology of the Civil War—like Lee's offering his sword to Grant and Grant's handing it back and Jefferson Davis's fleeing from the Federals disguised in a woman's clothes—that Seymour was a treacherous Copperhead who connived at the New York City draft riots of July 1863. These events, so far as I know, had never been reliably put on record till Stewart Mitchell, an authority on New York State politics, published, in 1938, his biography of Horatio Seymour. The draft riots of '63 were provoked by the federal Enrollment Act, which was decidedly unfair to the poor, since, although it had been framed with the purpose of allowing exemption for men with large families or in positions of responsibility, it also permitted the well-to-do to buy themselves off from service by hiring a substitute or paying three hundred dollars. New York City had already then a large foreign-born population—especially of the Irish—who, from reading the Democratic papers, were prejudiced against the government. The draft was supposed to include all able-bodied, foreign-born males between twenty and forty-five who intended to become citizens, and when the names were drawn of those who were thus drafted for an immediate three-year service, a good many of them rebelled. So far from wanting to fight for the Negroes, they were savagely embittered against them, since these former slaves had been fleeing to New York and competing, as was thought, for their jobs. They lynched a number of Negroes and burned down a colored orphan-

age, as well as murdered several whites and burned a
suburban block.

Horatio Seymour, at the time, was on his way to spend
a weekend in Long Branch, New Jersey, but he immediately returned to New York. He had never been a
Copperhead in the sense of someone who was totally opposed to the war. Although he wanted the conflict settled
by compromise, he had loyally supported the union and
been active in raising troops. He had protested against the
suspension of habeas corpus and the more and more disturbing interference with the freedom of press and speech.
He had opposed the Emancipation Proclamation—as had
a number of other people—on the quite correct constitu-
tional ground that such a measure could not be taken by
the action of the executive alone, without the approval
of the people, and he now, incorrectly, opposed the draft
on the ground that it was unconstitutional. He demanded
that its constitutionality be investigated and ruled upon
and, in the meantime, its enforcement deferred; and he
insisted that the Republican authorities were exacting dis-
proportionate quotas, in comparison with those of New
England, from certain New York districts which were
known to be Democratic. As a result, these injustices were
ironed out and the enforcement of the draft was—though
only very briefly—delayed. It was reported in the Republican press that Seymour had egged on the rioters from
the steps of the City Hall, but this, it seems, is entirely
untrue; the rioters were three miles away from the City
Hall. The people that Seymour addressed were a random
crowd of passersby. He urged his hearers to restrain themselves, and he called out the militia to keep order. There
were few federal troops in the city, for they had mostly
been sent to Pennsylvania, where the battle of Gettysburg
had just been fought.

But Seymour was made a victim of the furious fanaticism of wartime. He was denounced as a renegade, a traitor, an agent of Jefferson Davis. He was actually a cool, independent man with a strong sense of moral principle—resented by George Templeton Strong, that peevish and heated Republican, for what he called Seymour's smugness—and an unperturbed Democrat in a period of Republican ascendancy. The population of New York State consisted at that time of the long-established Dutch and the settlers from New England who in the last sixty or seventy years had moved as far west as this—together with a later-arriving admixture of Germans and Irish. Even the former New Englanders, now enjoying, in the vast spaces of that sparsely peopled countryside, a new freedom from the constrictions of New England bigotry and the tightness of New England towns, did not necessarily carry the fever of the Calvinist abolitionists from among whom they had emigrated. True, Utica produced Gerrit Smith, who financed the mad homicide John Brown, but it was also the home of Seymour, who did not believe in abolition, though, believing in free speech, he had defended the abolitionists when they were being hooted down at a meeting in Utica. The very looseness of the New York communities, and their remoteness from one another, made agreement and consistency difficult.

From this background and this situation, the Civil War stories of Frederic derive a unique historical as well as a literary importance. The hero of "The Copperhead"—really a short novel—is not merely a critic of Republican policies but a real out-and-out dissenter, a farmer whose ideas are rooted in the principles of the American Revolution and who believes that the South has the right to secede. He is ostracized and persecuted by his neighbors, but then, when the conflict is over, they realize they have injured a man who ought to have commanded respect, since he has stuck to his conviction of what was just and

has braved the hysteria of the war years, and they unite
in rebuilding his house, which had been burned in a raid
against him. (It was and still is a custom in that part of
the world for the neighbors to turn out and help to rebuild
a house or a barn that has burned.)

The other stories are, in various ways, reliable records
of the place and the time. They are distinct from most
fiction written after the war not only in their dramatiza-
tion of the conflicting feelings aroused by it but also in
dealing mainly with the civilian population at home.
There are very few glimpses of the armies in the field. "A
Day in the Wilderness" is the only one—and it is not one
of the best—which is occupied entirely with soldiers on
active service. There is in general no melodrama, no romance, and very little sentiment. The anguish and bitterness caused by the disruption of domestic life and the
discordance in once quiet communities is treated with a
sober and ironic restraint. The call of the bugle is heard,
but from afar and not always irresistibly. In the story
called "The Deserter," even the deputy marshal at home
feels sympathy for the outlawed boy who has been hired
as a substitute but has run away from the army to look
after his ailing old father. Pretending to shoot at the fugi-
tive, he allows him to escape to the forest. In "Marsena,"
one of those lethal coquettes who figure so prominently in
Frederic's fiction sends a mild and harmless suitor to his
death by challenging him to compete with a stronger,
more dashing rival, whom she has also incited to enlist.
She gets herself to the war as a nurse, and finding both
her former suitors seriously wounded and the weaker one
dying, she hardly condescends to recognize them, for she
has found better game in the person of a fatuous and
dandified staff officer who has received only a minor in-
jury.

Two of these stories came out in the *Youth's Com-*

*panion,* and they seem to have been written for boys, but all avoid Civil War clichés, and they stand as acrid first-hand testimony to the delusions and lasting grievances inflicted on American society by that fracture which, in the course of the recent centenary, was so much misinterpreted and so much romanticized.

The next working of Frederic's regional field was his first really successful novel, both artistically and from the point of view of sales: *The Damnation of Theron Ware* (called in England *Illumination*), which appeared in 1896. We are still in upstate New York, but we are introduced to characters of a different kind from those who have figured in Frederic's earlier fiction. They are at once on a higher level—men of exceptional intellect, a woman of aesthetic sensibilities—and more mercilessly treated by the author, with an almost complete disregard of the contemporary literary conventions. The book attracted much attention both in England and over here. The story was run off with the smoothest skill; the author had been at work on it five years. It was amusing, absorbing, rather shocking. It dealt in the coolest way with those problems of religious faith which had already, with more emotion, been made the subject of novels and poems. It was the kind of book that everybody read. A young Methodist minister—Theron Ware, married but with no children—comes to the pulpit of an upstate town. This town, which is given a classical name, Octavius, like so many of the towns of New York, is not really to be identified with Utica, because Utica was at that time a city of something under forty thousand, whereas we are told that Octavius had a population of only ten thousand. For this reason, the few highly intelligent people have to depend much more upon one another. The learned Catholic priest has come to dine twice a week with an equally learned doctor, who has now retired from practice in order to

conduct scientific experiments, and he has also made a
friendly alliance with a beautiful and cultivated Irish girl
—Celia Madden, the daughter of a peasant father, a
wheelwright who has made himself rich as the owner of
a wagon factory. She believes herself a votary to the Greek
ideal and, though insisting she is really a pagan, enjoys
playing the organ in the Catholic church. Theron Ware
is sufficiently sensitive and, though ill-educated, sufficiently educable to come under the influence of all three
of these people, who, themselves being hungry for com-
panionship, take a special interest in him. They become,
as it were, his three tempters. The priest, though quite
faithful to his duties and though he predicts that the
United States will eventually, on account of the quarrel-
ing among the Protestant sects, find it more comfortable
to become Catholic, is sophisticated in the extreme in regard to the origins and the nature of his Church and
casually disturbs for the first time the Methodist faith of
Theron, a subversion to which the doctor further con-
tributes by his materialistic atheism. The minister is an
eloquent preacher, and he has already been antagonized
by one of the trustees of his church, who has warned him
against bringing "book-learnin' or dictionary words" to the
pulpit or "puttin' in organs an' choirs" and who has told
him that his "wife'd better take them flowers out of her
bunnit afore next Sunday"—an admonition to which
Theron has cravenly submitted. His demoralization is completed by the redheaded Irish girl, who makes up to him,
takes him to her rooms, and, with a background of repro-
duced Greek statues, plays the piano and saturates him
with Chopin—who does, in fact, everything but literally
seduce him. He becomes dissatisfied with his wife, with
whose own aspiration toward beauty, as manifested by the
flowers on her bonnet, he has been bullied into interfering, and he decides he must abandon the ministry. His

Protestant hostility to the Catholic Church has been shaken not merely by the urbanity of the priest but also, on a crucial occasion, by his having had an opportunity to contrast the wrestlings with Satan of a Methodist camp meeting with the jollity of a Catholic picnic, its gay music and baseball and beer. This outing has been made romantic by its having been followed by a walk in the woods with Celia, at the end of which she kisses him.

Many readers, including myself, though they have followed this novel with fascination, cannot help finding it rather repellent. A rereading makes the reasons for this plain. The three tempters, though Celia and the priest are presented not without sympathy, do really behave rather badly. They all put on performances for Theron in a way that shows little consideration for a green young man they are supposed to like. Why, for example, is Father Forbes, who is presented as the last word in Catholic sophistication and must know about Methodist doctrine, made to begin talking about "this Christ-myth" only the second time Theron has met him? This is surely neither behavior becoming a priest nor elementary good manners. And why, in the midst of this, should he talk in a perfectly irrelevant way about Lucretius foreshadowing Darwin? Is this Frederic himself showing off or Frederic making the priest show off? And then why should Dr. Ledsmar, unless with malevolent purpose, have made a point of sending Theron a translation of Renan's *Souvenirs d'Enfance et de Jeunesse?* (It must have been due to Frederic's own ignorance that he also makes the doctor send him a volume of Renan "which appeared to be devoted to Oriental inscriptions." The only work of Renan's which could possibly answer to this description is the *Corpus Inscriptionum Semiticarum,* a scholarly compilation of the Institut de France which Theron would not have been able to read and which the doctor would hardly have had in his library.) Celia Madden should surely have been able to size Theron up well enough to know that when she refers to "Meredith," he would hardly have known about George Meredith. He thinks she means Owen Meredith, the once popular author of *Lucile,* of whom Theron *has* vaguely heard. When they see what is happening to Theron as a result of their "illuminating" him, all three wash their hands of him with cold contempt and without a word of pity or counsel. The "damnation," also, is made to take place with what seems improbable speed. Though Theron's weaknesses have been shown from the start—his cowardice and his impracticality—is it plausible that in a mere six months Theron's face, as Celia's brother is made to say, should have ceased to give the impression of "the face of a saint" and to seem "more like the face of a barkeeper"? When Theron follows Celia to New York City, full at the same time of nasty suspicions of her relations with Father Forbes and of daydreams of going with her to Europe on a yacht supplied, presumably, by her money, she dismisses him and crushes him in what is surely— though it has never been suggested that this rather conceited girl is remarkable for a kindly nature—an unnecessarily bitchy way. It is impossible, it seems to me, at the present time to agree with Harry Thurston Peck, who said when *Theron Ware* came out that it was "a literary event of very great importance." I doubt whether a great novel can be written around a central character who, having once been made sufficiently attractive for the reader to share his emotions, is in the end so abjectly humiliated. It is true that Sister Soulsby, the half-charlatan Methodist "debt raiser," whose sympathy and common sense provide the redeeming element among Theron's mischief-making friends, does rescue him from his "damnation" by finding him a job in Seattle, to which he sets out with visions of using his exceptional oratorical gifts to get himself elected to the Senate, but the effect of the book is unpleasant. It had appeared in Frederic's novels that, unlike his respected Howells, he took a harsh sort of relish in producing confrontations which would give rise to quarrels and insults. Though Frederic, as his talent develops, is becoming more and more a master of a clear and impartial kind of comedy, there is a certain sour flavor in all his work, which perhaps, although certain of his books in their time could not fail to attract attention, has kept them from being much read since.

Yet Frederic himself, from all accounts, though he was capable of bullying and truculence, was remarkable for good-natured high spirits and usually possessed by enthusiasm for some idealistic cause. There is a passage at the beginning of *Theron Ware,* when Theron has not yet come to Octavius, in which Frederic ascribes to him a state of mind that must have been characteristic of himself. For Theron, "the period was one of incredible fructification and output. He scarcely recognized for his own the mind which now was reaching out on all sides with the arms of an octopus, exploring unsuspected mines of thought, bringing in rich treasures of deduction, assimilating, building, propounding as if by some force quite independent of him. He could not look without blinking timidity at the radiance of the path stretched out before him, leading upward to dazzling heights of greatness." (This is not a good example of Frederic's prose.) An intellectual and imaginative expansion was to go on in an astonishing way all through Harold Frederic's life. It is this kind of "illumination," transferred to the mind of a somewhat loutish boy from the farm, which he projects into Theron Ware. But Frederic was not so loutish and, though brought up on Methodism—his family had been active in the Methodist Church—he had himself no stake in religion. He makes Theron Ware soon come to grief, but Frederic himself had gone on to more and more illumination and more and more worldly success. It should be noted, however, that at the same time that Theron is in this state of expansive euphoria, he is running into serious debt, and that this kind of disregard of consequences was also characteristic of the career of Theron's creator.

I have said that one of the most striking features of Frederic's New York State fiction is the accuracy and completeness with which he covers these communities. As a reporter for the Utica *Observer,* he had written about everything from art exhibitions to the gruesome crimes of the countryside, and when he went on to write its editorials, he became an expert commentator on politics. He qualified himself by reading and local tradition to write about the Revolution as well as the Civil War, of which he had also kept the firsthand impressions of a very observant child. And he was now, during his years in Europe, to demonstrate his capacity for acquiring through study and through personal experience a knowledge of the history, the structure, and the habits of living and thinking of any social or national group to which he turned his attention. An experienced newspaperman whom he consulted in New York on his way to London describes him, says Paul Haines, as "uncouth and awkward in 'a long green overcoat that made him look like a cucumber'" and "mainly anxious 'about the etiquette of the steamship, not at all about his press functions after landing.'" But he soon seemed to get the hang of London almost in the same way as he had known the ins and outs of New York, and he became one of the most searching and most alert of American foreign correspondents. He followed British politics with a diligence that sometimes surprised the English, had Burke's *Peerage* at his fingers' ends and was able to bring it up to date, familiarized himself with the slums and the criminal low life of London.

He informed himself at first hand about current affairs by dining with and entertaining the journalists and politicians, and became one of the liveliest members of the rather bohemian Savage Club, where he could always, it is said, hold the floor, up to the time he was asked to resign in consequence of having cabled to the *Times* the contents of an as yet unpublished book of Swinburne's which had been lent him by another member. Swinburne's copyright was thus destroyed, and the two clubmen came to blows. Frederic then joined the National Liberal Club, but was still received at the Savage. (Gertrude Atherton says, in her memoirs, that he is supposed to have assaulted John Lane, the publisher, in an argument about money, as a result of which the latter had to spend several days in bed.)

Frederic also covered Europe and Russia. Two of his series of articles were published in book form, in 1891 and 1892: *The Young Emperor: William II of Germany* and *The New Exodus: A Study of Israel in Russia*. The second of these is much better than the first. It is probable that Frederic's German blood made him overrate Wilhelm II—though at that time, in the United States, the admiration for modern Germany, which seemed in some ways so like America, was carried to extravagant lengths. A novelist's sense of character gave Frederic some imaginative insight into the personality of the Kaiser, but what he takes for Wilhelm's liberalism under pressure of labor disturbance and the rise of the Social Democrats excites him, after three years of Wilhelm's reign, to write that, though "the future may be tempestuous and discoloured by fire and blood," it may, "far better, be a gentle story of increasing wisdom, of good deeds done and peace made a natural state instead of an emergency in the minds of men." He praises the German Army as the greatest that the world has ever seen and seems to be unaware of the dangers of Prussian militarism. He is said, however, in conversation, to have made the prediction to an English friend "that the armed peace of Europe would be exploded by 'some idiot in the Balkans . . . with a bomb or pistol shot at some useless Kinglet . . . into the goddamndest hellfire ever imagined . . . and don't you fool yourself into the belief that we all—British and Americans —will get off scot free. We'll all be in it.'" *The New Exodus* is a much more convincing job, because, as Mr. Haines has shown in his extracts from Frederic's articles on the cholera epidemic, his reporting is more effective when he is telling about what he has seen. Harold Frederic spent two months in Russia and, without knowing the language, succeeded, through translations and interpreters and by firsthand observation of what was going on, in more or less penetrating the murk and confusion which are so likely to blot out Russia from the rest of the world. He broke the appalling story, which the censorship had tried to suppress, of the hounding and dispossession and banishment of tens of thousands of Russian Jews. In *The Return of the O'Mahony*, a romance which followed this book—though, with its absurdities of Gothic gimmickry and its extremely implausible plot, it is by far Frederic's weakest novel—he does, also, show real knowledge of Ireland, a country in which he had become interested when he discovered the Irish in New York State. He had frequently visited Ireland when he lived in England; and he wrote for the *Times* some articles so strongly pro-Irish that the editor tried to make him tone them down. (It is probably important in this connection that Kate Lyon's mother had been a Mahony.) He had visited French Canada in the eighties, and what he wrote about it shows that he had sized up its situation in a way then and now uncommon for visitors from the United States. In an article on "The Race Question in Canada," he said that the priests there exploited the farmers. "The future must turn upon the ability of the priests to hold their people. If they had a tithe of the sense and tact of the Irish priests in the States they could do it. But they are narrow, intolerant, ignorant men as a class, and the drift is all against them. And the moment the beam tips their way, snap will go the Dominion!"

As the power, then, of Frederic's mind had gone on from a Utica paper to exercise an influence in state politics, so it now went on from New York State to the comprehension of Britain and Europe. The author of the memoir already quoted says of Frederic that he "admitted one day, when challenged, that, after having seen what real world politics meant, nothing would have tempted him to go back to America and take up his pen again in the squalid struggle for a living at the public expense that is called politics in America." And where a Fuller or a Henry James looked on from the fringes of Europe, Harold Frederic plunged into its life, participated in its movements. It is plain from his notes for his books and from the scheme of *Theron Ware* itself that he had soon come to think in terms of the larger conceptions of Western thought. And as an American from upstate New York, he suffered from few inhibitions. "All these years of the nineties," wrote Frank Harris on Frederic's death, "Frederic was growing rapidly, but it was primarily the American in him which appealed to me from the first—a power of judging events and persons on their merits, heedless of position or apparent importance."

It was for a long time a serious error on the part of American criticism to disparage Frederic's English novels. Ernest Sutherland Bates, in the *Dictionary of American Biography*, says of them that, "written in failing health and during domestic trouble, they add little to his reputation." (Actually, *The Market-Place* was a best-seller in

1899.) And even Van Wyck Brooks brushes off these
books in *The Confident Years* by declaring that Frederic
"lost himself . . . as a novelist in his foreign surroundings, and he seemed to bear out the rule that Howells laid
down for his disciples, 'Write about the life you know
best.'" But Frederic had evidently exhausted the material
of the life he had known at home; he had nothing more
from there to write about. Yet it is important to note that,
in his subsequent novels, the central figure is, except in
one instance (in whom, however, there is also an American element), either a transplanted American, an Englishman who has lived in the United States, or one who has
grown up abroad and just come for the first time to England. Harold Frederic has simply gone on to utilize his
own later experience. This is a Frederic now immersed in
English life but still unmistakably American.

In the novels he is henceforth to write, Frederic's mimicry of English, Scotch, and Irish speech seems, at least to
a non-British reader, almost as faithful as his expert ren-
dering of the speech of his various kinds of New Yorkers.
The little book *Mrs. Albert Grundy: Observations in
Philistia,* which he published in 1896 in a series called
"The Mayfair Set"—when he had been in England twelve
years—is a curious tour de force. It exactly catches the
tone—coy humor, snobbish chitchat, light discussions of
subjects of general interest—of the writings of G. S. Street,
who also contributed to this series. At the other extreme
of history, in a pair of short stories that are made to take
place in the Middle Ages, Frederic brings to the Wars of
the Roses the same kind of practical grasp and carefully
exact description as he does to an Oneida County turkey
shoot or a Methodist camp meeting. When he came, in
*The Market-Place,* to deal seriously with modern England,
I learn from Mr. Austin Briggs, it was the American reviewers, not the English, who complained that Frederic's
knowledge of English life was only superficial.

Of his later books, three are light potboilers—*Mrs. Grundy, The O'Mahony, March Hares*—though I agree with Mr. Briggs that the last of these, and the most amusing, probably reflects Frederic's state of mind, melancholy and disillusioned, when he had not yet accomplished much and, in its love story, the stimulating excitement of his discovery of Kate Lyon. Two more serious books came out after Frederic's death, which occurred in 1898—two years after *Theron Ware*—when he was only forty-two. The first of these, *Gloria Mundi,* is not of Frederic's best, but ambitious and rather surprising. Frederic is trying here to deal with the pressure of modern change on the hereditary structure of England. It is very much the kind of thing that Shaw was already writing and that Wells was later to write. Frederic's notes for it show the range of the problems that he contemplated attacking: "Big Estates, Business, Man at 40, Religion and Education, Art, The Sex Passion, Woman, England, The Army Set, and Children." A young man called Christian Tower, who has grown up in France, falls heir to a great ducal estate and comes for the first time to England, which he sees, as Frederic had, with the eyes of an English-speaking foreigner. His grandfather, the Duke, is a brutal old man, dying in a room full of rank-smelling dogs. He says of a local farmer who has barred him from riding through his property, "A good hearty cut across the face with a whip is what'd teach swine like Griffiths their place—and then let 'em summons you and be damned." He represents the barbarity of feudal England, which is tenacious but now on its last legs. One of Christian's cousins, who has Jewish blood, is aware of the cruelty to the tenants and serfs which has maintained the Duke's position, and he has tried to atone for it on his own estate by inventing what he calls "the System." This is a limited utopia of fifteen square miles inhabited by two thousand people. They are made to work at medieval crafts, for which the estate itself provides most of the raw materials. The aim is to isolate them from the modern world and to regulate their lives in such a way as to make everybody happy. When Christian suggests that this is socialism, his cousin is horrified and indignant, and it presently becomes apparent that this artificial community is almost as much at the mercy of the discipline imposed by its master as the serfs had been enslaved by theirs. Christian cannot accept this solution any more than he can acquiesce in the tyranny of his feudal grandfather, but, after the Duke dies, he cannot see any way out of taking on the responsibilities of the great estate. He does, however, violate tradition by marrying a London typist, an independent and intelligent young woman of the kind to which belong so many of the heroines of Wells and Shaw. The reader is left wondering what point Frederic wants to make. Is it simply that it is difficult for the landed nobility to dispossess themselves?

The second book, *The Market-Place,* is connected with *Gloria Mundi* and evidently intended as a counterpart to it. Though Frederic has studied and documented himself on the life of the aristocracy, *Gloria Mundi* is rather unreal. *The Market-Place* is closer to what he has lived. It is perhaps, after *Theron Ware,* the best of Frederic's novels. Here the half-alien central character, Joel Thorpe, is the son of a London bookseller and an adventurer who has been away fifteen years. From living for some time in America, he has got to talk like an American and is sometimes mistaken for one. He is what we call nowadays an "operator," and completely unscrupulous and unashamed. The novel is the story of his struggle with the London Stock Exchange—his disasters when he is outswindled and his outrageous successes in outswindling the swindlers. In the end, he has made a fortune by selling stock in a rubber plantation in Mexico. When taxed with this property's worthlessness by someone who knows about it, he replies that, for his own purposes, the plantation might as well not exist. He exploits the nobility, whom he double-crosses, and outwits the Jewish financiers. Having become in his travels an excellent shot, he can qualify in England as a sportsman. By his animal vigor and verve, he induces a Lady Cressage to marry him—an impoverished, somewhat shattered former beauty who has already appeared in *Gloria Mundi*. Her companion—Celia Madden, from *Theron Ware*, who has inherited her father's money and has left Octavius for Europe—takes a very much shrewder view of him and says that "crime was his true vocation." But having set himself up as a country gentleman, he finds himself restless and bored, and decides to get himself into Parliament. Despising the philanthropists as duffers, he has a vision of the possibilities of a demagoguery that would pretend to aim at the improvement of the miserable masses. His wife now "beheld in his face, as she scrutinized it, a stormy glow of the man's native, coarse, imperious virility, reasserting itself through the mask of torpor which this vacuous year had superimposed." The young Duke from *Gloria Mundi* appears in the last chapter. Thorpe makes a crafty effort to interest him in his project, which the Duke comments on as "interesting" but to which he does not commit himself.

The merits of *The Market-Place* lie not only in its elements of adventure but also in the psychological interest of the specious rationalizations and the pseudo-benevolent sentiments with which the predatory Thorpe tries occasionally to justify to himself the more and more callous skulduggeries into which his drive for power is dragging him. Theron Ware was an unself-flattering version of Harold Frederic as a young provincial eager to widen his social, aesthetic, and intellectual scope and to make for himself a career. Joel Thorpe is a similar version of Harold Frederic, the man of the world and the international journalist who has been able to go from conquest to conquest.

Harold Frederic had, at this point in his own career, arrived at the height of his powers. He was generally regarded as an important writer, and Scribners was about to bring out a uniform edition of his fiction. He was planning in his next novel to return to the American Revolution and to tell the story from the point of view of a Hessian mercenary—he had had one among his ancestors —who would figure as "a big swaggering bully," despising both the British and the colonists. But like Theron, he was now deep in debt, and he was loaded with domestic burdens. He had to support two households—two women and seven children. (It seems to me rather amusing, as an example of Frederic's insouciance, that his villa in Surbiton, where his wife lived, should have been called Oneida Lodge, and his second house, in Surrey, Homefield.) He now wanted to give up potboilers and journalism and concentrate on his serious fiction, and remembering Hawthorne, he applied to Oscar Straus, a man with whom he had the connection that they had both worked for Cleveland, for the consulate in Liverpool. Straus promised to try to help him, but he was never given the post —perhaps on account, Mr. Briggs says, of the disorder of his private life. In the meantime, he heavily overworked and, in August 1898, had a stroke. The doctors advised him to rest and to adapt himself to more temperate habits, but he dismissed their admonitions with scorn and went on smoking cigars, drinking brandy and whiskey, and riding. Kate Lyon was a Christian Scientist and called in a woman healer, who, Frederic said, "bores my head off." He became confused in his mind, insisted, like Dickens just before his death, that he was going up to London, gave self-confident opinions on foreign affairs, and bewildered a friend by asking, in his last hours, "Have you got that job done for poor Sullivan's daughters?" He died on October 19, 1898. He was cremated, and his mother had his ashes sent back to Utica, where he was buried in the Forest Hill Cemetery.

Frederic's death caused much trouble and scandal. He had made a will dividing his property equally between his two families, but actually they were both left penniless. Stephen Crane and his wife, close friends of the Frederics in England, took Kate and her children in. Petitions on behalf of both families were circulated by their respective friends. Bernard Shaw contributed five pounds for Kate's, with some especially tart remarks: "We have three very expensive orphans on hand already—parents alive in every case. My impulse is to repudiate all extra orphans with loud execrations. . . . I should simply take them out into the garden and bury them"; and Henry James, who had signed an appeal, contributed the same amount, writing, "Deeper than I can say is my commiseration for those beautiful little children." When Cora Crane sent James *The Market-Place,* he wrote her that he had read it "with a lively sense of what H. F. might have done if he had lived—and above all lived (and therefore worked) differently!" But Grace Frederic's faction brought a charge of manslaughter against Kate Lyon and her Christian Scientist healer—a charge that was quite unjustified. The evidence about this is confused. It seems certain that Frederic had had two qualified doctors and refused to take their advice. To one of them, he had replied, "You order what you like, and I'll take what I like." But a close friend of his says that in his lucid moments he protested against the healer and demanded medical treatment. The case got into court, but the charge against Kate had been dropped and the other defendant was acquitted.

Certain aspects of this imbroglio have remained rather mysterious. Some light has been thrown on it by Mr. Haines and by the Stephen Crane letters and Lillian

Gilkes's biography of Cora Crane. But, as in the case of Henry Fuller, a full-length biography is needed. I understand, however, that all Frederic's books are soon to be made available in a good edition. A botched photographed edition, at a very high price, has already been issued. Here Frederic's first novel, *In the Valley,* and his third, *The Lawton Girl,* appear in a volume called *The Later Years,* and they are both wrongly dated as of 1900 instead of 1890. *Mrs. Grundy* is included in a volume of *Non-Fiction.* But an edition in fourteen volumes, under the supervision of Mr. O'Donnell, has been announced. In the meantime, there have been several reprints of *Theron Ware,* and the first complete collection of the Civil War stories. And a short but able study of Frederic by Mr. Stanton Garner has appeared in the University of Minnesota series of Pamphlets on American Writers.

June 6, 1970

# HOW NOT TO BE BORED
# BY MAURICE BARING

It is possible to read a good deal of Maurice Baring—his poetry, his plays, and many of his novels—and find him thin and insipid. I have had the experience, and I know very well how discouraging this writer can be if one comes to him in the setting of his generation—of Wells and Bennett, of Shaw, Chesterton, and Belloc. They were all of them friends of his, yet—except that the last two were Catholics—he seems to have had little in common with them. He, like them, did a great deal of journalism, yet he belonged to a different world, and it is difficult for the reader not to think of him as an aristocratic amateur. One has to adjust oneself to his constituting a very peculiar case before one is able to see how accomplished and able he was, and to know how to separate the Baring who was interesting from the Baring who may seem a phantom. The only book-length study of Baring so far has been the adoring memoir by his friend the singer Ethel Smyth. But Mr. Paul Horgan has now done him full justice in an admirable selection from his writings—*Maurice Baring Restored*—which shows his varied work at its best, and the long introduction to which covers the subject so competently that—embarrassingly for this reviewer—it leaves one little to add.

Maurice Baring's family in England was founded in the eighteenth century by a successful linen manufacturer, the son of a Lutheran pastor in Bremen. The sons of this German immigrant created the famous banking firm of Baring Brothers, and the Barings came to hold high office, sit in Parliament, and be raised to the peerage. Maurice was a younger son of the first Lord Revelstoke. Despite his weakness in mathematics, he was eventually allowed to qualify, by reason of his qualifications as a linguist, for the diplomatic service. In the course of his duties, he was sent to a number of important capitals, but he says that he "loathed" the service, and he resigned from it in 1904 and became a foreign correspondent for the London *Morning Post*. His long career as a journalist and the inferior quality of some of his books—he seemed to make books of everything he wrote, and some of them overlap—suggest that he must have been at least partly dependent on his writing for a living. He never married and he became a Catholic, and one feels that, in spite of much frequentation of the social and official worlds, he was something of an anomaly there, as he was also a sort of intruder into the professional literary world, where his friends read the books he sent them, which were sometimes dedicated to them, but did not quite regard him as one of themselves. His easy cosmopolitanism, his extraordinary gift for languages, and his fascinated sojourns in Russia, though they gave him intimate knowledge of so many things, both political and literary, were such as made him seem not even quite an Englishman; and his writings take so many forms and deal with so many subjects that he must present a troublesome problem to the conventional literary historian.

I agree in general with Paul Horgan about the relative

importance of Baring's works. The four departments I
would recommend are (1) his eight books about Russia,
of which only the two small volumes on Russian literature—he evidently stopped writing about Russia on the
eve of the 1917 Revolution—are still in print. Maurice
Baring was perhaps the only Englishman who really
knew the country well and who was also an excellent
writer. *The Mainsprings of Russia* and *The Russian People* are probably the best surveys of the history of Russia,
the best analyses of Russian society that had at that time
been published in English. They may seem today a little
old-fashioned—the author speaks often of "the Russian
soul"—but anyone who is interested in Soviet Russia
would find it worthwhile to read them, for written before
the collapse of old Russia, they show how this had been
led up to and how similar, after all, conditions under the
czar were to conditions under the present government.
Baring had lived so much in Russia and seen all classes at
such close quarters at the front during the war with Japan
and in Moscow during the 1905 Revolution that he seems
to have got to know it better than any other country, including England. In his *Landmarks in Russian Literature,*
of 1910, and *An Outline of Russian Literature,* of 1914,
as well as in his *Oxford Book of Russian Verse,* of 1925,
he performed for the English a service similar to that
which that other Russophile from the diplomatic service,
the Vicomte Melchior de Vogüé, had done in his pioneering book *Le Roman Russe* in 1886. Maurice Baring introduced the great Russian writers to the British at a time
when even *The Brothers Karamazov* had not yet been
translated into English—Constance Garnett's translation
appeared only in 1912—and it was possible for George
Saintsbury, who knew no Russian, to be condescending
about them. It is amusing that Vogüé, though he does
write admiringly about Pushkin, praising him as "the

Peter the Great of literature," had announced that he did not want to dwell on the poet, because he could not illustrate his merits by examples of his *"langue de diamant,"* untranslatable into French; because Pushkin is universal, only accidentally Russian; and because— though the Slavophiles will not like Vogüé's saying so— Pushkin is a typical romantic, like Byron or Lamartine, and does not, except in a very few poems, "reveal any ethnic character." Baring, on the other hand, again and again tried to disabuse the English-speaking world of the notion that one of the greatest of the poets of his age was a kind of diluted Byron. He has written the most accurate appreciations of Pushkin that I have ever seen in English.

My second recommendation of the Baring that is worth reading is his long novel called simply *C.* I have read a number of Baring's novels. They all display his intimate knowledge of the international social world, the wide range of his cultural interests, and his dry, end-of-the-century wit. He always knows how to touch off the incidental people of his novels: "On the Saturday on which Wright had been invited there was a typical gathering at Bramsley: the Bishop of Barminster, who had married a cousin of Lord Hengrave's, a florid and alarmingly condescending ecclesiastic, with a large beard and a fund of anecdote, whom Lady Hengrave thought transgressed the code of decency by being High Church. He wore a large gold cross, which she thought 'odd,' and he turned to the east when he said the Creed in church, which she said was against the law. With him was his apologetic, blond, and explanatory wife." All these books carry one along and hold one's interest to the usually pathetic end. But I have found that I cannot remember most of them only a few days after I have read them. The characters are pale, seem mere names, sometimes hard to distinguish from one another. They are, in fact, so little differentiated that one can rarely recognize the same characters when they turn up in different books. The chronicle of their social life becomes so monotonous and tiresome that one sometimes wonders what effect their creator is aiming at. We are invariably told who all the guests at all the dinners were and who sat next to whom, and a chapter is likely to end, "Then he turned to Lady —— on his left." When Baring wants, as he frequently does, to break off relations between his people, he can always have them shifted to another embassy or make them go somewhere else for their health. Is this due to an obsession on Baring's part with the kind of life he describes? The imputation of being too fond of this life seems to have been the only criticism to which he was at all sensitive—as in his reactions to a letter from Vernon Lee, quoted by Ethel Smyth, and in reproaches to Pushkin for his waste of energy in an addiction to worldly frivolities. We wonder, in reading *Cat's Cradle*, whether the author may not be trying to underline the dreariness of the social life that muffles the tragedy of the heroine. One sympathizes with Vernon Lee when she tells him that she does not find this novel "anything like as good as *C.*," and continues, "Even the English part seems to me inordinately full of trifling detail without realisation of the chief figures. (The men are all interchangeable.) But—but—but—you have somehow, and perhaps by this very thinness of texture, contrived to give an extraordinary essence of passion, rather like what music gives. . . . Of course I *dislike* your people, personally. I dislike their mixture of footling uselessness and devouring passion (they have *time* for it, as they never do anything but go to parties) and I dislike their (and your) Catholic other-worldliness: I abominate such making light of life and its . . . well! *uniqueness*." Vernon Lee acknowledges also that "these (in my eyes) poor, footling, paper puppets . . . have the quality of Tristram or Guinevere or Francesca, and that is . . . well, it's *great*." But one feels that the lack of intensity or emphasis does sap the effectiveness of most of these novels. (To Baring's plays, the lack of climax is fatal. Beerbohm said of a production of *The Grey Stocking* that Baring was "adramatic," and Shaw's enthusiasm for this play and the unproduced *His Majesty's Embassy* was evidently due to his valuing them as destroyers of popular illusions about upper-class social life and the diplomatic service.) Maurice Baring's principal themes are the Catholic religion and love. Yet we never understand the inevitability of the conversion of the principal characters, or of Maurice Baring himself, and we never can movingly imagine the passionate relations of his lovers, which are invariably buried at such depths of discretion. In *Cat's Cradle,* we wonder why Bernard, who has been so much in love with Blanche, does not pounce on her as soon as he sees her again. But in Baring's novels nobody pounces, any more than the characters are allowed to be seen at moments of religious revelation; nor would the ladies allow themselves to be pounced upon any more than the lovers would be capable of pouncing. Though, at the moment that I am writing, sex is being made so baldly explicit that it ceases to be attractive, we cannot but feel that Baring's novels need at least a touch of Lady Chatterley. They are, however, usually doomed to be long-protracted tales of frustration. The heroine marries the wrong man or is a Catholic and has scruples against getting a divorce, or the hero, as in *The Coat Without Seam,* is unable to bring himself to take advantage of the opportunities offered him. This undoubtedly was one of the causes—as in the case of Henry James, whose lovers are always renouncing—of the lack of popularity of these novels in relation to Gals-

worthy's or Wells's. And they do not even seem much to
have impinged on the consciousness of the literary world,
of his brother and sister writers. One finds very few
comments on them. Arnold Bennett notes of *Cat's Cradle*
in his diary that "its curious fault is that it reads as if it
really had happened: a report of actual events." Virginia
Woolf notes of *C.* in her diary, "Within its limits, it is
not second rate, or there is nothing markedly so, at first
go off. The limits are the proof of its nonexistence. He
can only do one thing; himself to wit; charming, clean,
modest, sensitive Englishman. Outside that radius, and
it does not carry far nor illumine much, all is—as it
should be—light, sure, proportioned, affecting even; told
in so well bred a manner that nothing is exaggerated, all
related, proportioned. I could read this for ever, I said.
L[eonard] said one would soon be sick to death of it."
Mr. Horgan's description of these novels, more careful
and more sympathetic than mine, is the most illuminating
that has yet appeared.

Yet *C.* is by far, it seems to me, the best novel of Baring's of those I have read. It contains his two most mem-
orable characters: Leila Bucknell, the irresistible siren
and invincibly successful bitch, who manages to be
financed by a succession of lovers without losing her
position in smart society; and Lady Hengrave, the hero's
mother, who represents everything most correct, most self-
confident, and most discouraging in the solid upper-class
world. Though *C.* himself, in love with and betrayed by
Leila, and tactfully thwarted by his mother, is the in-
variable Baring hero, delicately responsive to music and
poetry, who comes to a sad end, both these ladies are
treated with a good deal of humor and are really fine
comic creations. *C.* is too long for inclusion in Mr. Horgan's selection, and he has done well not to try to excerpt
it, except for one incident, and, instead, to reprint the

whole of one of the shorter novels—*The Lonely Lady of Dulwich*. This is a typical Baring story of misplaced and unhappy love. Mr. Horgan has also done well to include the Max Beerbohm parody " 'All Roads . . .' " which was added to a late edition of the *Christmas Garland*. It is a perfect quintessence of Baring: the flat, simple declarative sentences, the memories of a sensitive childhood, the international social occasions, at which everyone speaks several languages and someone sings delightful French or German songs and at which what the reader takes for the buildup to an exciting love affair ends only in the exquisite lady's having cured the so modest hero of a childhood dislike of Christmas. In Baring's own *Daphne Adeane,* the exquisite central lady, though much talked about and admired by way of a portrait, is never allowed to appear at all. She has died before the story commences.

The third department of Baring's writing that I want to commend to the reader is the sequence of burlesques and parodies that he published between 1910 and 1913: *Dead Letters, Diminutive Dramas,* and *Lost Diaries*— later reprinted in one volume as *Unreliable History.* One of the favorite devices here is to make the famous figures of the literature or history of whatever country or period talk and behave like the English characters of Baring's contemporary novels. Thus Catullus's Lesbia, writing from Baiae to a girl friend in Athens, and Charmian, writing of a dinner in Rome, are made to sound exactly like Leila Bucknell, and Lady Macbeth, writing to Lady Macduff, to invite her to stay at the castle and, if possible, bring her little boy, maintains the dignified, friendly tone of Lady Hengrave reasoning with C. to dissuade him from marrying a Catholic: "I am sorry to say Macbeth is not at all in good case. He is really not at all well, and the fact is he has never got over the terrible tragedy [the murder of Duncan] that happened at Inverness. At first I thought it was quite natural he should be upset. Of course very few people know how fond he was of his cousin." Goneril writes to Regan as follows: "We have been having the most trying time lately with Papa, and it ended today in one of those scenes which are so painful to people like you and me, who *hate* scenes." In an interview with a Greek traveler, the Emperor Nero—speaking Greek, as the visitor says, a little too well—depreciates Roman art in comparison with the Greek, laughs and shrugs when the traveler says he has heard that the games in the Circus are "extremely well worth seeing." To go to them, says Nero, is "part of my profession," but "if I had my own way I should witness nothing but Greek plays acted by my own company in my own house." He regrets, when the visitor is going, that the Empress Mother—whom her son has in fact just poisoned—is "suffering from one of her bad attacks of indigestion" and unfortunately cannot receive him. The Athenians at a smart dinner, in *After Euripides' "Electra,"* say all the banal things that the Londoners would have said: "Poor Euripides! He's shot his bolt," and "What I say is this, that Clytemnestra thoroughly deserved to die, but Electra wasn't the person to kill her, and that as she did kill her mother she ought to have been punished."

Another of his best burlesques, "Sherlock Holmes in Russia," not included among these selections, appeared not in the "History" series but in a volume called *Russian Essays and Stories.* Baring says that it owes much to a young Benckendorff, who was a great Sherlock Holmes fan and had wondered how Holmes would have got on in Russia. In this story, Holmes has Watson accompany him to the country house of a prince to which he has been invited. A number of things have been stolen. Holmes succeeds in retrieving some of them but discovers that the son of the household is a dedicated revolutionary, who has introduced bombs into the household and has had some of the saucepans taken away, apparently in order to disguise the transference of half a million rubles for the revolutionary cause. The village policeman does not arrest the thief, of whose identity he is perfectly aware, and Holmes questions him: " 'But if you know he did this, why don't you arrest him?' I asked. 'God be with him, no,' replied this astonished and astonishing policeman. 'Why arrest him? He has already been in prison once.' 'What for?' I asked. 'He killed the brother of the gamekeeper . . . and he stole hens.' . . . 'Does the Prince know this?' . . . 'Of course he knows it.' . . . 'Then why does not he insist on his arrest?' . . . 'The Prince has pity on us. . . . We are poor people. If he were arrested he would soon come back again and probably kill me; he would certainly burn my house.' " The situation is seen to be complicated and becomes baffling even to the English Holmes, who, although he speaks Russian perfectly, cannot understand Russian behavior. In the end, a little score book for the game of skat, the disappearance of which has been worrying the household, and which Holmes believes to have been used by the son to write revolutionary messages in cipher, turns up unexpectedly in a drawer of the card table. Holmes, says Watson, after leaving Russia, bewildered and badly vexed, "never referred to the matter again, nor does he like any mention made of the game of skat."

The fourth section of Baring's work that cannot be disregarded is that of his literary criticism, with which must be considered his anthologies. These latter are of a peculiarly personal kind. They include his two volumes of *Algae*, which he subtitled "Anthologies of Phrases," and his last substantial book, *Have You Anything to Declare?*, a compilation of favorite passages from a lifetime of multilingual reading. The *Algae* consist of very short bits of verse and prose from the literatures of eight languages. By isolating these lines and phrases thus and giving each one a page, he lends them a special distinction—as Eliot does the passages he borrows or quotes—of which one may not have been aware if one has met them in rapid reading. Maurice Baring's own poetry is not very impressive. His early lyrics are like old-fashioned undergraduate verse—too many sighs and roses, lilies and asphodels, too much unevocative reference to gold and silver and the sun and the moon and the stars—and his later long elegies on the death of friends and of a nephew, which have sometimes been much applauded, seem to me uninterestingly conventional. Yet in his sonnets one occasionally finds lines which might perhaps satisfy the taste that compiled these fastidious anthologies:

> —And when the moon compels the storm to cease
> And calms the wind; and all the skeins of foam
> Unravel softly on the vanquished sea.

> —Like a sad pilgrim who has wandered far,
> And hopes not any longer for the day,
> But blinded by black thickets finds no way,

> Comes to a rift of trees in that sad plight,
> And suddenly sees the unending aisles of night
> And in the emerald gloom the morning star.

> —I shall not see the faces of my friends . . .
> In those dark nights before the summer ends;

> Nor see the floods of spring, the melting snow,
> Nor in the autumn twilight hear the stir
> Of reedy marshes, when the wild ducks whir
> And circle black against the afterglow.

Baring's two collections of essays, *Lost Lectures* and *Punch and Judy,* have, no doubt because their tone seems rather casual, been undeservedly neglected. He is particularly good on French literature. He says, on the whole correctly, that the lack of appreciation of French poetry on the part of English critics—A. E. Housman once asked a French writer why French poetry had no magic —is due to the prime disadvantage of their not understanding French prosody. One may not be able to agree with him that La Fontaine is the greatest French poet, but if you want to understand what the French admire in their poetry, you cannot do better than read Baring on Racine or his review of *The Oxford Book of French Verse*. *Have You Anything to Declare?*, which he calls a "notebook with commentaries," also shows Baring at his best as a critic. He begins by saying that he once dreamed he had died and, after crossing the Styx, was confronted by a Customs House official with *Chemins de Fer de l'Enfer* on his cap. He was handed a printed list of not the usual dutiable articles but all the principal literary languages. The favorite passages that follow, not all of them as short as those in the *Algae*, extend from Homer to Belloc and Chesterton. I have read in this book many times. It would, I should think, be worth studying— though not perhaps in a college course—by anyone with literary ambitions. Baring was a fine connoisseur of writing and an excellent guide to style.

And Mr. Horgan is a sure guide to Baring, giving us the best of him in most of his departments and following his example in compiling, in a section called "Good Things," some of his author's witticisms and throwaway sayings. Since the reviewer of a book of this kind should always be able to regret the inclusion or omission of something, I may say that, instead of "The Alternative," a fantasy of scrambled history, I should have preferred one of the weirder episodes from the volume of short stories called *Half a Minute's Silence*, such as the tale of the two modern Englishmen who find they have landed, on their way to the Canaries, on the sinister island of Circe. The only section included here that shows Baring at his least impressive is the first part of *The Puppet Show of Memory,* in which he tells us about his childhood and gives us nothing but trivial memories—Christmas pantomimes and Christmas parties, home theatricals and made-up games—but which is warranted, on the threshold of Mr. Horgan's book, by reason of the fact that it establishes Baring in his cultivated and comfortable, very well-to-do family environment. The chapter on Eton in Baring's book differs strikingly from the accounts of George Orwell and Cyril Connolly, for Maurice Baring seems never to have been flogged or bullied; he appears to have been quite happy throughout his youth. His friend Max Beerbohm has once again put his finger on the slightly absurd aspects of Baring in the caricature of him in the series of the "Old and New Self." Here the mature Baring, ruddy, glaring, and in evening clothes, with a copy of *The Puppet Show* in his hand, to which he points emphatically and anxiously, appears like a bugaboo at the bedside of his uninterested little-boy self, who is trying to go to sleep, reposing on two soft pillows: "Old Self: 'Now, my little dear, *you* mayn't remember everything you've been and gone and done and thought and seen today. But *I* do. And before you go to sleepy-bye I'll read it to you.' " But these memoirs, which tell us almost nothing about his parents and brothers and sisters, his religious experience or his love affairs, become a good deal more interesting in his accounts of his diplomatic travels and of his adventures during the war in Manchuria and in St. Petersburg after the revolution of 1905.

The photographs of Baring and Max's caricatures are curiously out of keeping with the fine vibrations and the alert sense of humor that one finds in the best of Baring's books. And these books, although infused with a sense of comedy, never carry practical joking and compulsively violent behavior as far as Baring did in his life. For we are told that he liked to startle by setting fire to his scanty hair, by jumping into the Thames with his clothes on, or by leaping up and hanging by a chandelier. He would walk through a smart Paris restaurant at the time of the Dreyfus case (though he said that he detested the Dreyfusards) shouting, *"Dreyfus est innocent!,"* throw his eyeglasses into the fire when some lady said she did not like them, or fling an expensive overcoat out of the window of a railway compartment when he found that he could not get it into his valise. One of his more amusing pranks was riding on a bicycle to a country house to which he had been invited for a weekend, taking off his hat, as he passed, to the people at the front door expecting him, and disappearing till the following evening, when he punctually turned up for dinner. He called himself a troll, and I believe that his impulses to do something unconventional at variance with his deadpan appearance were protests against the world of Lady Hengrave and the routines of the country house and of the diplomatic service, in the latter of which he once frightened into collapse one of the women who worked in the office by sending her, compressed in a dispatch box, one of those snakes that pop out. He seems to be protesting thus against his own dignified presence, as he is in his parodies of solemn speeches and official justifications. I believe that a certain defiance of the well-bred British assumptions contributed both to his adherence to the Catholic Church and to his fascination with Russia, where, during the Manchurian war, he suffered severe hardships and mingled with all classes of people, as he would never have done in England. But this *esprit de contradiction* is usually very quiet and itself appears quite well bred. It is only when one catches its flavor that Maurice Baring becomes entertaining, and only if one responds to what Vernon Lee calls the musical charm of his writing that one can become mildly addicted to Baring. The troll-like element in his personality, though it more or less muted his emotions, did not prevent him from becoming a very shrewd man of the world or, throughout the First World War, from functioning ably as a staff officer in the Royal Flying Corps. But one remembers him not as the block-like books that fill up the shelves of one's library or as the solid dreams those books project but as the varied conversation, at times almost opalescent, of a very pleasant companion, whom it is always refreshing to listen to, even if one may not always remember exactly what it was he said.

September 18, 1971

# THE AFTERMATH OF MENCKEN

In the spring of 1912, just before graduating from prep school, I somehow happened to pick up a copy of the *Smart Set,* a trashy-looking monthly, and was astonished to find audacious and extremely amusing critical articles by men named Mencken and Nathan, of whom I had never heard. I continued to read the *Smart Set* through college, at first with a slight feeling of guilt, for it was making fun of everything respectable in current American drama and literature. But the "American Renascence" had already begun, and I was already dissatisfied with the traditional critics. I had never paid any attention to William Dean Howells in *Harper's,* and *The Nation* was dominated by Paul Elmer More, who seemed to be opposed on principle to any contemporary of talent, whether American or English. When, at college, I discovered a book by W. C. Brownell called *American Prose Masters,* it was with a hope (because that was a time when we wanted American literature taken seriously; as was said of Noah, we prayed for rain and were deluged), a hope which was followed by disappointment. Brownell disapproved of Poe, and though it was he who, as an adviser to Scribners, had had them bring out the New York Edition of Henry James, he did not seem really much to believe in him. He had, as I learned afterward, rejected Van Wyck Brooks's *America's Coming-of-Age,* which was eventually to become a landmark, on the ground that it was still "too early" to call attention to the weaknesses of our supposed classics. But Mencken, quite outside the New England tradition, to which he was sometimes unfair, was not constrained by its inhibitions and was honestly attempting to sift out what was valuable from the rubbish of our own very second-rate period—from the eighties to the early 1900's —and as he became more self-confident in his heresies he steadily became more impressive. I was led to reread *Huckleberry Finn* and to look up *What Maisie Knew,* which Mencken had described as "a passionless masterpiece."

The strange history of the *Smart Set* has been told in detail and most entertainingly by Mr. Carl R. Dolmetsch in his *The Smart Set: A History and Anthology,* with a personal memoir by S. N. Behrman. The magazine was founded by Colonel Mann, the blackmailing owner of *Town Topics,* as "the Magazine of Cleverness," and was then aimed at an appeal to social rather than intellectual snobbery. It became involved in Colonel Mann's scandals, but was later bought by someone more respectable and edited by Mencken and Nathan and Willard Huntington Wright—that somewhat mysterious character who began as a high-powered intellectual but later turned into "S. S. Van Dine," the popular writer of detective stories. It was abandoned by Mencken and Nathan in 1923, when the then owner forbade them to print a disrespectful squib about President Harding's funeral train, and fell into the hands of Hearst, who dropped it at the time of the Depression. This history

has now been followed by a volume of Mencken's con-
tributions to the *Smart Set, H. L. Mencken's Smart Set
Criticism,* very well selected and edited by William H.
Nolte. This last cannot, of course, carry with it all the
atmosphere of the old *Smart Set,* which was something
quite special, created by the unique combination of the
editors with the magazine's variegated past. There was
the cover, with its young man and woman in evening
dress, he bowing, she curtsying with a fan, watched from
the background by a masked devil, who was snaring
them with long strings prettily baited with winged hearts.
As the magazine became more and more a vehicle for the
editors' ideas and for superior stories and poems, this
cover became incongruous; it underwent many transfor-
mations in order to bring it up to date, but it basically
remained the same and came to seem one of the jokes
of Mencken and Nathan, who were informal and reck-
lessly mischievous. They had a department called "Ameri-
cana," in which they reprinted absurdities from the press,
and another called "Répétition Générale," which was
devoted to ideas and epigrams that they thought they
might use later. There were dialogues, in which each
wrote his own lines and in which they were represented
as walking along Fifth Avenue or in some other local
setting. They invented a character called Owen Hatteras,
to whom some of these features were sometimes ascribed;
he was supposed to have become a major in the First
World War and was afterward given that rank. Owen
Hatteras was the purported author of a pamphlet called
"Pistols for Two," in which actually each of the editors
was writing—sometimes fantastically—about the other.
"He dislikes," wrote Mencken of Nathan, "women over
twenty-one, actors, cold weather, mayonnaise dressing,
people who are always happy, hard chairs, invitations to
dinner, invitations to serve on committees in however

worthy a cause, railroad trips, public restaurants, rye whisky, chicken, daylight, men who do not wear waist-coats, the sight of a woman eating, the sound of a woman singing, small napkins, Maeterlinck, Verhaeren, Tagore, Dickens, Bataille, fried oysters, German sou-brettes, French John Masons, American John Masons [John Mason was then a well-known American actor], tradesmen, poets, married women who think of leaving their husbands, professional anarchists of all kinds, ven-tilation, professional music lovers, men who tell how much money they have made, men who affect sudden friendships and call him Georgie, women who affect sudden friendships and then call him Mr. Nathan, writ-ing letters, receiving letters, talking over the telephone, and wearing a hat." "His table manners," wrote Nathan of Mencken, "are based upon provincial French prin-ciples, with modifications suggested by the Cossacks of the Don." Mencken had been trained as a journalist on the Baltimore Sunpapers, and so was never oppressed by the American academic standards, which he contin-ually ridiculed and denounced. And even as a journalist he was very much at his ease. On one occasion, limited for space, he cut off an article in the middle of a sentence.

One finds in Mr. Nolte's selection the original reviews, then so unconventional, of Conrad, Huneker, and Dreiser which were afterward used as material for the solider essays of *A Book of Prefaces*, of 1917. I am glad to find old pieces I remember and that Mencken never collected —especially the summaries of periods in his life, such as the "Taking Stock," of March 1917, written to celebrate the occasion of his "one hundredth mensual discourse in this place," in which he tells us that in the course of the eight and a third years he had "grown two beards and shaved them off; I have eaten 3,086 meals; I have made more than $100,000 in wages, fees, refreshers, tips, and bribes . . . I have been called a fraud 700 times, and blushed at the proofs . . . I have had seventeen proposals of marriage from lady poets . . . I have been abroad three and a half times, and learned and forgotten six foreign languages . . . I have fallen downstairs twice . . . I have read the *Police Gazette* in the barbershop every week; I have shaken hands with Dr. Wilson; I have upheld the banner of the ideal; I have kept the faith, in so far as I could make out what it was," etc., etc. This frankness had the effect of making the *Smart Set* pleasantly informal: you might almost have been drinking with him at Lüchow's. It is at once funny and rather irritating to find this old German Nietzschean in one of his favorite Nietzschean phrases, describing Anatole France as "still fit for dancing with arms and legs." How else is it possible to dance? But can one imagine either Nietzsche or Mencken or Anatole France performing any such antics as this suggests? Mencken, however, got tired of the *Smart Set*—as he said, of its gray paper, its cheap format. The *American Mercury* followed, a much more attractive-looking production. It was this that most people, I think, read when Mencken's reputation was at its height. But it was otherwise not as attractive as the *Smart Set.* The break with Nathan left it deficient both in humor and in what Mencken called "beautiful letters," and the writers on current affairs tended all to give the impression of having been so processed by the editor himself that their work seemed practically to have been written by him—an impression which he later tried to explain away as having been created by the necessity he found himself under of remedying the bad writing of many of them. And it is therefore very much worthwhile to have Mr. Nolte's collection of Mencken's earlier, more spontaneous work.

There is in English no satisfactory biography of

Mencken, no sound, comprehensive book. Van Wyck Brooks's chapter about him in *The Confident Years* is, from the literary point of view, the best thing I know. I was interested to hear Brooks say that he thought it was one of the best things he had ever written. His and Mencken's temperaments were so much unlike that this makes it a great tribute to Mencken's influence. *The Irreverent Mr. Mencken,* by Edgar Kemler, and *Disturber of the Peace,* by William Manchester, are both undistinguished journalistic jobs (the second much fuller and more valuable than the first). *H. L. Mencken: A Portrait from Memory,* by Charles Angoff, who worked with him on the *American Mercury,* has its interest as a personal memoir but gives a disagreeable impression. It seems obvious that Mr. Angoff was a rather humorless young man and that Mencken was constantly kidding him—he called Angoff "Professor"—and that Angoff is having his revenge in very much the same way that Anatole France's secretary Jean-Jacques Brousson did in his books on his late master. This Mencken is made to sound like a wisecracking, insensitive bully talking nonsense at drunken parties or, in his office, propounding outrageous opinions that one feels, when one has gauged Mr. Angoff's intelligence, must have been specially intended to shock him. The daughter of a Baltimore friend of Mencken to whom I lent Angoff's book said that she was quite unable to recognize the man who used to come to their house. I find difficulty in believing, as Mr. Angoff asserts, that "it was no secret that during a great part of their relationship they [Mencken and Nathan] were little better than friendly enemies." It is true that the partners broke up over the policy of the *Mercury*—Mencken's ambitions as a serious thinker were, I believe, getting a little beyond him—but it was only at the time of the *Mercury* that Angoff knew the editors, and their friendly relations

were later restored. My impression on the few occasions
when I visited the *Smart Set* office was that they worked
together in their comedy act, in person as well as in
their writings, on a not at all inimical basis. Mencken
was likely to be carried away into developing one of his
paradoxes, irrelevant to the business in hand, in a way
not much different from that of his written monologues,
and Nathan would cut short his digression by interjecting
some brisk little question of a more or less illogical kind
which would stop his partner in his tracks. It would
take Mencken a moment to grasp it, and there was no
way to make a sensible reply.

But there does now exist in French a large-scale study
of Mencken that is superior, as far as I know, to anything else that has been written: *H. L. Mencken—
L'Homme, l'Œuvre, l'Influence,* by Guy Jean Forgue, a
professor at the Sorbonne, who formerly worked at Yale
and has edited a volume of Mencken's letters. Though
written in French for the French, this study attacks the
subject in a more serious and scholarly way than any of
the books by Americans. M. Forgue goes into Mencken's
origins, German as well as American, and analyzes, in
relation to them, his ideas and his attitudes, which
present so many contradictions, with the systematic thoroughness so characteristic of French criticism and a sense
of the American background that is astonishing in a
foreigner. He explains the importance to Mencken of his
immigrant Prussian grandfather, who was proud of his
relationship to the Bismarcks and looked down on other
Baltimore Germans; the grandson was an enthusiastic
Nietzschean, adored German music to the exclusion of
other kinds, wrote an admiring article about Luden-
dorff at the time of the First World War, loved to talk
about the *Polizei* and the *Gelehrten,* and idealized the
German nobility. His opposition in both the wars to the

championship of England by the United States and
his interest in the "American language" in contradistinc-
tion to the English were evidently the results of his loyalty to Germany. Mencken was a curious example of the
second-generation American who, in the freer life of
the United States, retains the strong social prejudices of
the people that he still belongs to, though his family have
left them behind, and the situation in his case is complicated by the Menckens' having come to the South, so
that Henry liked to defend the Confederate cause in its
quarrel with the Washington government. His strong col-
loquial flavor and knockabout verbiage cannot be conveyed in French, but it is remarkable that a Frenchman
who has lived in this country for a relatively short time
should appreciate these so well and translate them as
accurately as he does.

And we have also now a memoir of Mencken which
brings us closer to his personality than any other has yet
done and which should be read as an antidote to Angoff:
*The Constant Circle: H. L. Mencken and His Friends,*
by Sara Mayfield. After the death of Mencken's mother,
with whom he had lived all his life and on whom he was
much dependent, he married, at the age of fifty, Sara
Haardt, also of German origin, and set up a new establishment. Sara Haardt was already gravely ill, and she
died, five years later, of tubercular meningitis. She grew
up in Montgomery, Alabama, and Miss Mayfield was a
close friend of hers from her girlhood. Miss Mayfield's
book deals primarily with this episode in Mencken's life,
and her story is interesting in several ways. Besides pre-
senting a unique intimate record of the private personality of Mencken, which M. Forgue so carefully
distinguishes from the legend of himself he created, Miss
Mayfield gives a lively account of the Montgomery in
which she and Sara Haardt and Zelda Sayre (later Fitz-

gerald) and Tallulah Bankhead grew up. Montgomery
had been the first capital of the Confederacy; Jefferson
Davis had taken the oath of office in the Capitol. The
girlhoods of Zelda and Tallulah are described as having
been just what one had always imagined. They were
both the daughters of important local citizens: Zelda's
father and Miss Mayfield's father were associate justices
of the Supreme Court of Alabama; Tallulah's was a con-
gressman, and an uncle a senator. In New York, they
gave the impression of young barbarian princesses from
a country where they were free to do anything—though
Miss Mayfield tells us that Tallulah was eventually sent
away to an Academy of the Sacred Heart to keep her out
of trouble. I recognized the type in bud when I once
came up from the South on the train, sitting across from
a pretty blond belle in rolled stockings with her feet on
the opposite seat, who played jazz on a phonograph all
the way. She might have been Tallulah or Zelda in the
phase described by Sara Mayfield. Zelda, says Miss Mayfield, "two years younger than Sara, was still tomboy
enough to stride the guns [of the Capitol], slide down the
banisters of the famous circular staircase in the rotunda,
and climb over the minié balls, piled up in pyramids like
oranges in the fruitstands." "Her only rival" was Tallulah
Bankhead, who "could bend backward far enough to pick
up a handkerchief from the floor with her teeth, stand on
her head, and turn a fancy cartwheel," as well as imitate
one of their teachers—who wore high net collars and
long black dresses and attempted "by prim bearing and
quaint methods . . . to instill the aristocratic manners of
the old school into us"—"in a way that made us rock
with laughter." Tallulah was genuinely witty and Zelda
had some literary ability. Sara Haardt, "fragile, lovely,
and flame-like," was less obstreperous and was more
serious-minded. Like Miss Mayfield, she went to Goucher,

where they both wrote short stories. Through these short stories, a prize for one of which Sara Mayfield won in a contest in her freshman year, these girls got to know Mencken when he came to make the award and spoke to them on "How to Catch a Husband." Apart from her Saxon ancestry, her having grown up, like him, in the South, and her interest in literature, Mencken must have been attracted to Miss Haardt by something of the same kind of charm—which Miss Mayfield says was irresisti- ble—that made Zelda and Tallulah popular. She be- came a regular solace and companion of Mencken after his mother died (the talkative bachelor's indispensable woman friend), and though he fought marriage off for a time, having avoided and disparaged it all his life, it was inevitable that he should marry her. Miss Mayfield, in telling about this, brings out Mencken's considerate and sensitive side in a relationship which seems to have been unique for him. He was certainly much shaken by Sara's death. One had the impression after this that he was left more disagreeable and bitter, becoming rather nasty in his arguments with such opponents as Upton Sinclair, in a way that had not been characteristic of his hard-hitting but good-humored ridicule. Sara died in 1935, and the situation was made for him much worse when his ideal of Germany was contradicted by the be- havior of Hitler and the Nazis, of whom Mencken had never approved but of whom he had always predicted that the Germans would soon get rid.

This memoir by Sara Mayfield is well done and a valuable document. It is a good thing that someone has survived to write it. (I must protest at a small point, how- ever. A story has persisted from volume to volume—I find it also in Manchester and elsewhere—that "with the diary [Zelda's] in hand, Scott [Fitzgerald], Edmund Wilson, and John Peale Bishop besieged Nathan in his apart-

ment in the Royalton until he finally invited them in to
have a drink." As for my own part in this alleged exploit,
I never saw Zelda's diary, I barely knew George Nathan
—at that time I had not even met him—except in connection with some articles that he wrote for *Vanity Fair*,
and I was never in his apartment in the Royalton. I do
not think it at all likely that he would allow himself to
be "besieged"—he was a pernickety and snubbing little
man—or to behave in the expansive way that, in another
version of this story, he is made to. Now that I am old
enough to see biographies of people I remember and
descriptions of occurrences that I knew at first hand, I
have come more and more to distrust the statements
found in writings on literary figures on which the authors
have been unable to check. I have even been inaccurate
myself—as I have found on consulting my journals—in
my memoirs of old friends. Did Trelawny tell the truth
about Byron and Shelley? Was Edmund Gosse reliable
about Swinburne? Later investigators say definitely not.)

When Mencken died in 1956, after his years of dis-
ablement and silence, he was cheerfully looking forward
to the publication of a book which he had got together
before his stroke and later, after his stroke, forgotten till
it was found by his secretary. This was *Minority Report:
H. L. Mencken's Notebooks,* published in the year of his
death. It is a scattering of reflections on all sorts of subjects tossed off in the course of years. "It will be nice to
be denounced again," Miss Mayfield reports him as saying. In spite of my great admiration for Mencken, which
is usually revived when I reread him, this book, when
first I read it, rather repelled me. Here you have to take
account inescapably of his habitual confusion in thinking
and his dogmatic German brutality. In a note, at the end
of the volume, on the development of his own style, he
declares that "the chief character of my style . . . is that

I write with almost scientific precision—that my meaning is never obscure." It is true that *Minority Report* is written in plain enough English, with little Menckenian embroidery, but the statements in the methodically numbered paragraphs do not always hang together, and since they are rendered clearer than usual by the simplicity with which they are put, we are relatively little distracted by the writer's tremendous entertainment value. On one page, he is recommending that, although the Pure Food and Drug Act is "falling into the hands of uplifter-bureaucrats" and "bound to become arbitrary and oppressive," it is "sound in principle" and should require "that everything for human ingestion that is offered for sale should show a label indicating its ingredients." On another, he lays it down that "No one ever heard of the truth being enforced by law. Whenever the secular arm is called in to sustain an idea, whether new or old, it is always a bad idea, and not infrequently it is downright idiotic." He is always demanding freedom, but he regards as "one of the most irrational of all the conventions of modern society . . . the one to the effect that religious opinions should be respected." This convention protects the theologians, with whom one would first have to deal (what does this mean? Aren't all religious opinions theological?), "so they proceed with their blather unwhipped and almost unmolested, to the great damage of common sense and common decency. That they should have this immunity is an outrage." Should religious opinions not acceptable to Mencken therefore be whipped and molested—that is, should they be suppressed? What else can you do about them? After all, one is not forced to accept them. "If all the farmers in the Dust Bowl were shot tomorrow, and all the share-croppers in the South burned at the stake, every decent American would be better off, and not a soul would miss a meal." Note the use of "decency" and "decent" in the last two of these quotations. One may admit that it is uncomfortable to hear about the poor and that any great solicitude about human life, except where oneself is concerned, has lately gone by the board, if it ever widely existed. But will decent people really be gratified and "better off" at hearing about other people being burned at the stake?

Mencken's attempt to stave off such criticisms as this is to be found in item 429, where he argues against his critics: "If you were against the New Deal and its wholesale buying of pauper votes, then you were against Christian charity [which Mencken often told us he was]. If you were against the gross injustices and dishonesties of the Wagner Labor Act, then you were against labor [which Mencken very often was]. If you were against packing the Supreme Court, then you were in favor of letting Wall Street do it. If you are against Dr. Quack's cancer salve, then you are in favor of letting Uncle Julius die [Uncle Julius is evidently a German]. If you are against Holy Church, or Christian Science, then you are against God [the whole idea of a Divinity has been discredited on another page]."

These paragraphs, then, after all, are not so very much different from the jottings in the "Répétition Générale" in the pages of the old *Smart Set*. But these contradictions are so obvious that they have never really mattered. We never expected coherence of Mencken. He was a poet in prose and a humorist, and in his time, in certain departments, one of the bringers of light to "the Republic."

May 31, 1969

# AN EFFORT AT SELF-REVELATION

It is almost impossible to describe the new posthumous Hemingway book, *Islands in the Stream*, from the point of view of what happens in it without making it seem preposterous. It gives us Hemingway as a concoctor of self-inflating fantasies at his most exhibitionistic. You have him in his Cuban residence, very thinly disguised as a painter, one Thomas Hudson, showing his sons how things ought to be done and how to behave like men (his younger brother Leicester has explained how Ernest liked to instruct him); you have him in his favorite bars, where he can bully his hangers-on, subjecting them to his sarcasm and otherwise putting them down, and as captain of his own boat, maintaining a good-natured but effective discipline among a gallant crew that adores him. All this time, he is being brought drinks by his servants, by the waiters, or by the members of his crew. One of the last, who drinks too much, is wisely and firmly checked, and in a moment of equally firm self-discipline Hudson makes the dramatic gesture of throwing "high over the side" and letting "the wind take it astern" a glass of "gin and coconut water with Angostura and lime." In his relations with

other people he is always on top, always the acknowl-
edged "champion" that Hemingway aspired to be in his
writing when he boasted that he was "trying to knock
Mr. Shakespeare on his ass." The most outrageous de-
parture from plausibility, which is also the weakest of the
episodes, occurs when Hudson's first wife, long divorced
and now a singer entertaining the troops, makes a point
of looking Hudson up and eagerly goes to bed with him.
This woman is not in any way recognizable as Hemingway's first wife but all too recognizable as a well-known
friend of Hemingway's. But why, one asks, if these two
characters in the novel can enjoy such passionate love,
did they ever separate? They are agreed not to talk about
the past; they acknowledge that they were both to blame.
But why can they not be reunited? Nothing is ever explained.

It has always surprised me that the more or less imaginary Hemingway, the myth about himself that he managed to create by the self-dramatization of his extensive
publicity and, in his fiction, by the exploits of some of his
heroes, should have imposed on the public to the extent
it did. The grumbling or bristling reaction on the part of
certain reviewers to Mr. Carlos Baker's biography, which
took account of the petty and cruel and ridiculous aspects
of his subject, makes it plain that the ideal Hemingway
was a living reality to many of his admirers. It is true that
he was capable of courage, that he was capable of doing
certain things very well. But actually, from the beginning,
it was not merely the exploits of his heroes, athletic or
sporting or military, that made his best stories compelling;
it was the strain they conveyed of men on the edge of
going to pieces, who are just hanging on by their teeth
and just managing to maintain their sanity, or of men who
know they are doomed to inexorable defeat or death. The
real heroism of these characters is their fortitude against

such ordeals or the honor they manage to salvage from ignominy, humiliation. It is this kind of theme in Hemingway that makes his stories exciting and stimulating. Will the hero last? How long will he last?

Now, with all its preposterous elements, this imperfect work, *Islands in the Stream,* makes one feel the intensity of a crucial game played against invincible odds as one has not quite been able to do in connection with any of his last three finished novels—*For Whom the Bell Tolls, Across the River and Into the Trees, The Old Man and the Sea.* It has never been pulled tight or polished, as Hemingway would undoubtedly have done, for his sense of form was exacting. Everything goes on too long, even the most effective episodes: the boy's struggle with the monstrous swordfish—which he loses; the hunt for the Germans among the reefs at the time of the Second World War—which results in Hudson's being shot by them. The barroom conversations are allowed to run on to a length that has no real point and in the course of which our interest slackens. These would all—if Hemingway had taken time to treat them with his characteristic technique —have surely been condensed to far fewer pages. That he knew well how much work there was still to be done is made clear by Mr. Baker's quotations from his letters to Charles Scribner. *The Old Man and the Sea* and *For Whom the Bell Tolls* are more satisfactory from the point of view of form, yet they seem to me a good deal less interesting than *Islands in the Stream.*

They are less interesting because only here is Hemingway making an effort to deal candidly with the discords of his own personality—his fears, which he has tried to suppress, his mistakes, which he has tried to justify, the pangs of bad conscience, which he has brazened out. This effort is not entirely successful; hence, I imagine, his putting the manuscript away. You are never allowed to know exactly what has happened in Thomas Hudson's past. He is always admonishing himself that he must not allow himself to think about it, so in order to avoid this he orders a drink. The reader clearly sees the drink but not the memory that is being stifled. One is made to feel acutely, however, an ever-present moral malaise. The painful gnawing, amid jolly scenes of drinking, in affluence and beautiful weather, is perhaps more insistently here made to ache than in any of Hemingway's other books since *The Sun Also Rises*. There is something more than needlings of conscience; there is that certainty of the imminent death that has threatened in so much of his writing. And the book is given special force and dignity by one's knowledge of the writer's suicide. He invents for his own family, as they figure in the story, deaths that did not actually occur. Two of Hudson's sons are killed in a motor accident, and a third is killed in the war, whereas in reality, though Hemingway's boys were involved in a motor accident, they were not fatally injured, and one who had served in the war and disappeared for a time turned out to have been only taken prisoner. Hemingway himself was not shot by a German, like his hero in *Islands in the Stream*. He did not even ever come to grips with the enemy—though he had formerly suffered injuries so frequent that they seem almost to have been self-inflicted —in his one-man campaign against submarines. He died in retirement, by his own hand. It was the dread, the pressure, the need for death, the looming shadow, no doubt, of the memory of his father's suicide, that drove him so determinedly to meet it.

This book contains some of the best of Hemingway's descriptions of nature: the waves breaking white and green on the reef off the coast of Cuba; the beauty of the morning on the deep water; the hermit crabs and land crabs and ghost crabs; a big barracuda stalking mullet; a heron flying with his white wings over the green water; the ibis and flamingoes and spoonbills, the last of these beautiful with the sharp rose of their color; the mosquitoes in clouds from the marshes; the water that curled and blew under the lash of the wind; the sculpture that the wind and sand had made of a piece of driftwood, gray and sanded and embedded in white, floury sand. But to bunch in this way together these phrases of the section called "At Sea" is to deprive them of the atmosphere of large space and free air and light, of the sun and rain on the water, in which the writer makes us see them, and to see them always in relation to the techniques of fishing and navigation. Though the whole thing centers on Hudson and though Hudson is kept always in the foreground, there is a certain amount of characterization of his family and friends and retinue—especially in the case of the boys, with whom Hemingway can come closest to identifying himself. The ability to characterize with any real insight has never been Hemingway's gift. Of the surface of personalities he has always been very observant, and of voices and ways of talking he is a most successful mimic. In his book of reminiscences of Paris, he reproduces for one who has known them the hoarse British gasps of Ford Madox Ford, the exasperating nonsense of Scott Fitzgerald so faithfully that one can hear them speaking, and one can also hear the tones and turns of speech of persons one has never known. But one is made aware, particularly in *A Moveable Feast*, whose characters are real people, how little their friend—or companion—could actually have known about them: what was going on in their minds, what they were aiming at, what they were up to. And his judgments were almost always disparaging. He wanted to make everyone else look ridiculous or morally reprehensible. It was only Ezra Pound who escaped —rather surprisingly, since Pound had once been useful to Hemingway, and it was usually to the people who had helped him or to whom he owed something in a literary way that he was afterward to make a point of being insulting. But in *Islands in the Stream* he allows himself little scope for malignity. He is able to be fond of most of his characters, since they all respect and obey Thomas Hudson, are glad to be molded or guided by him. " 'Tommy,' " says his second in command, when Hudson is dying, " 'I love you, you son of a bitch, and don't die.' Thomas Hudson looked at him without moving his head. 'Try and understand if it isn't too hard.' . . . 'I think I understand, Willie,' he said. 'Oh—,' Willie said. 'You never understand anybody that loves you.' " This is sentimental and "self-serving," but it does show, perhaps, on Hemingway's part an attempt to take account of his noncomprehension of other people.

The mimicry of himself by Hemingway has also been mainly on the surface; the malaise itself has been kept there—sometimes, as in "A Clean, Well-Lighted Place," without any indication of what it is that is troubling the character. We are not even, as in "Big Two-Hearted River," told explicitly that there is any cause for disquiet, yet this idyll, which is simply an account of a solitary fishing expedition, is related to something in the background that is never even referred to, which makes the fisherman concentrate with special attention on every baiting of the hook, every catch, every cooking of the fish in the open air. That something, as Hemingway was later to explain, was the young man's experience of the war. Now, in *Islands in the Stream,* the experiences that have been pushed down out of sight are continually rising into consciousness; but not even here, as I have already said, are we told exactly what they are. In order to keep them out of his consciousness, Thomas Hudson takes another drink or plunges on into his program of action. Yet in spite of this, the mythical figure of Hemingway is constantly breaking down, becoming demoralized by the memory of past betrayals of women who have trusted and loved him, betrayals of his heroic idea of himself. The situation is made truly tragic by the fact that the mythical Hemingway did have a certain basis in reality. After all, he did not always fail or make a fool of himself, though he needed, I think, an audience, if of only one, to appreciate and applaud him. His triumphs were partly actual and were of a kind that, for his larger audience, seemed to satisfy two typical American ambitions: that of becoming an accomplished outdoorsman and that of making a great deal of money. What had been lost was a part of an ideal self that had partly been realized.

I do not agree with those who have thought it a disservice to Hemingway's memory to publish this uncompleted book. Nor do I agree with those who, possessed by the academic mania of exactly reproducing texts, declare that Mrs. Hemingway and the publisher should have printed the manuscript as Hemingway left it, without making the cuts she explains. The author is not to be charged with the defects of manuscripts which he did not choose to publish and for which he can now take no responsibility, nor his editors with making those works more coherent if the editing has been done with good judgment. I imagine that this book, in the long run, will appear to be more important than seems to be the case at present, and I believe that Mrs. Hemingway is to be encouraged to go on to publish further manuscripts.

January 2, 1971

# THE WASTE LAND IN DÉSHABILLÉ

There has always been curiosity about the early version of T. S. Eliot's *Waste Land*, submitted to Ezra Pound and to some extent altered by Eliot in accordance with Pound's suggestions. One had always imagined that it must have been preserved among the papers of John Quinn, the rich New York lawyer who acted as a patron to Eliot and acquired many of his manuscripts. This suspicion has turned out to have been correct. The manuscript has been found by a niece of Mr. Quinn's, Mrs. Thomas F. Conroy, who has sold it with other manuscripts to the Berg Collection of the New York Public Library; and it has now been published: *The Waste Land: A Facsimile and Transcript of the Original Drafts, Including the Annotations of Ezra Pound,* edited by Valerie Eliot.

An article on the subject had already appeared in the London *Times Literary Supplement*, which gave a very fragmentary preview. It was revealed that the poem was originally to be called *He Do the Police in Different Voices,* and this was soon identified (*TLS*, January 1, 1969) as derived from Chapter 16 of Dickens's *Our Mutual Friend,* in which Sloppy, a foundling, is employed by Betty Higden as a boy-of-all-work and reads aloud to her from some paper like the *Police Gazette,* apparently imitating the characters.

It is obvious that Eliot meant to refer to the different voices of the poem: Boston Irish, cockney, the literate English of the much-read young Harvard spokesman, brooding on his dissatisfactions, which recall many echoes from literature. But the result of this new discovery was to give a new priming to the pump of the Eliot industry. It was now said that, in order to grasp *The Waste Land* properly, it would be necessary not only to study the books which Eliot mentions in his notes, but to reread the whole of *Our Mutual Friend.* Is Sloppy the same person as the Tiresias of the poem? Does not water, especially the Thames, play a recurrent part in both *Our Mutual Friend* and *The Waste Land?* Is the dust mentioned in *The Waste Land* not connected with the dust piles of Mr. Wegg?

These speculations were carried to the point of absurdity and, in the course of a long correspondence lasting for three months, the allusion-hunters were rebuked by a Mr. Douglas Hewitt, who says sensibly that

A great deal of criticism of Eliot assumes that a quotation from another work implies that the whole of that work is to be borne in mind while we read the whole of the poem and that a complex unity will finally emerge from this accumulation of associations. . . . My argument is that Eliot often uses the quotations and echoes more locally than this. I suspect the cancelled title of being downright frivolous and I am appalled at the thought of all those forthcoming theses which will labor every parallel between the two works and misrepresent Dickens when he does not fit in with Eliot's vision.

The most obvious thing to say about this early draft of *The Waste Land* which was operated on by Ezra Pound is that Pound did extremely well with it, that he really produced from Eliot's rough version a more or less Poundian work more successful than anything on a similar scale he had been able to do himself. He saved Eliot from many ineptitudes. Here we see for the first time the long passage in heroic couplets which Pound induced him to cancel—though Eliot says that he himself thought them "excellent." "Pope has done this so well," advised Pound, "that you cannot do it better: and if you mean this as a burlesque, you had better suppress it, for you cannot parody Pope unless you can write better verse than Pope— and you can't."

This advice was certainly sound. One is astonished at the mediocrity of which Eliot was capable here. He was decidedly not at his best when he was trying to be arch and sophisticated. Pound also rescued Phlebas the Phoenician, whom Eliot had wanted to discard, and dissuaded him from printing "Gerontion" as a kind of prelude to *The Waste Land*. He checks Eliot's occasional uncertainty in some statement as to what is happening, reminding him that since the spokesman of the poem, Tiresias, is supposed to know about everything, the poet cannot himself be uncertain. On the other hand, he sometimes made recommendations which Eliot did not accept. He criticized as "too penty" one of Eliot's best lines.

> *Yet there the nightingale*
> *Filled all the desert with inviolable voice.*

The substitution of five syllables for a regular iamb here is masterly and what gives the line its magic.

It is curious to see Eliot hesitating and not hitting the nail on the head. Clive Bell said that Eliot's poems showed a wonderful instinct for "phrasing"—and so they do, but these drafts do not. It is not entirely Pound's advice which has pulled Eliot's lines so tight and given them so much significance even when allusions and borrowed words must be unrecognizable to many readers. This Eliot has done mostly himself; and it is striking that almost nowhere in these unfinished drafts or in the drafts of associated poems can one identify a single passage, even a single line, which is identifiable as Eliot's best.

The selection of what is to be kept has been made with unerring taste. The oddest excision, and one of the longest, is that of the beginning of the poem, preceding "April is the cruellest month," made by Eliot himself. The opening of the poem was originally a monologue, a little in the vein of Hemingway, in which a narrator, who is evidently Irish—since all the names are Irish and there is a snatch from an Irish song—seems to revert to a scene in South Boston. This narrator has got very drunk "at Tom's place" and goes to a brothel where a woman named Myrtle, who had been raided the week before and wants to retire to a farm, tells him he is too drunk and unshaved for any of the girls to go to bed with him, "but she gave me a bed, a bath, and ham and eggs." Leaving the brothel, he is picked up by "a fly cop," apparently for urinating in the street, but he is rescued by a man he knows, with whom he goes off in a cab. The cabman and another occupant of the cab get out to "run a hundred yards on a bet . . . so I got out to see the sunrise, and walked home."

This picture of vulgar demoralization is intended, I suppose, to set off the anguish of the cruel April and to associate itself with the "stony rubbish" from which the poet is longing to be delivered. It implies desperation and adds to the incoherence of the accents of hopeless despair and invincible impotence that follow. Phlebas ("Death by Water") is introduced by another long passage (mostly in blank verse) which was perhaps originally intended to

counterbalance the South Boston narrative and tells the
story of a fishing expedition off the New England coast:

> *Then came the fish at last. The eastern banks*
> *Had never known the codfish run so well.*

These American memories seem incongruous, sandwiched
in with the London impressions.

Bleistein of "Burbank with a Baedeker" puts in an unexpected and rather puzzling appearance as the drowned
man in a travesty of the Shakespearean "dirge" from *The
Tempest*:

> *Full fathom five your Bleistein lies*
> *Under the flatfish and the squids.*

Bleistein in the other poem is evidently a vulgar and well-
to-do Jew who gets the Princess Volupine away from
Burbank. But what exactly did Bleistein mean to Eliot?
In the "Dirge," it is said of him:

> *Though he suffers a sea change*
> *Still expensive rich and strange.*

Is his being left at the mercy of the fish intended to humiliate him, although the poet seems to feel for him a
certain lurking respect?

The somewhat related poems such as "The Death of
Saint Narcissus" have also been searched for good lines
exploitable in a better setting:

> *The wind sprang up and broke the bells*
> *Is it a dream or something else*
> *When the surface of the blackened river*
> *Is a face that sweats with tears?*

The whole composition of *The Waste Land* is a curious
and striking phenomenon. Pound and Eliot between them

have managed to concentrate an intensity of image and feeling which is not to be found in these drafts, where the brilliance of the finished work is nowhere in evidence. It is partly Eliot's instinct for drama, so much more effective here than it usually is in his plays, which makes telling the abrupt contrasts and the laconic notations and comments—an instinct which Pound in his *Cantos* in general fails to exercise. *The Waste Land,* remaining incoherent, is vivid; these drafts are extremely blurred.

Mrs. Eliot has been most conscientious and has practiced an admirable lucidity in disentangling this complicated text—a task which involved distinguishing between Eliot's own criticisms, those of his first wife, and those of Ezra Pound, which last are given in red. The only point which, so far as I know, has been omitted in the notes on the drafts, though Mrs. Eliot quotes the relevant passage from Dante, is the meaning of "Another" in Eliot's line "And if Another knows, I know I know not." Ulysses, in Dante, is referring to God: his ship is condemned to go down because he has been so impious as to venture beyond the Pillars of Hercules, the straits of the Mediterranean—*"com' Altrui piacque"*—but God's name cannot be pronounced in Hell. One assumes that Eliot's ship is also doomed. It seems to be heading for a precipitous shore:

*My God men there's bears on it.*
*Not a chance. Home and mother.*
*Where's the cocktail shaker, Ben here's plenty of cracked*
*   ice.*
*Remember me.*

And the drowned Phlebas immediately follows.

# "BALDINI"

## A Memoir and a Collaboration
## with Edwin O'Connor

When I first knew Edwin O'Connor in the late forties,
he was spending his summers near me at Wellfleet, Cape
Cod. He was working at a broadcasting station in Boston
and had very little money to spend on vacations. He lived
in a shack on one of the "ponds"—which to us non-
New Englanders seem more like "lakes"—with an equally
unaffluent friend, and he rode around on a bicycle. We
would see him on the beach writing, and he occasionally
came to call on us. When his first book, a short novel
called *The Oracle,* was published in 1951, he gave me a
copy and asked me to read it. It was a caricature of a
stuffed-shirt radio broadcaster, and although I was amused
by the ironic tone, I could not believe in the central
character as a genuine human being, nor did he quite
achieve the dignity of a striking comic creation. We did
not talk in those days about books very much, but we
discovered a common interest in amateur magic. We kept
up with the literature of the subject—I find that Ed
O'Connor had collected a considerable library, which was
almost exclusively technical, whereas mine ran considerably more to historical and biographical material. We

frequented magicians' supply stores and exchanged secrets of sleight of hand. At one point, Ed had acquired a new method of performing "the pass"—which "Professor Hoffmann," that curious Victorian broker who became the pioneer in English of literate writing on magic, has described as "the very backbone of card-conjuring"—that was smoother than the old-fashioned method but which I was never able to master. The same qualities that made Ed a raconteur who could hold the attention of any company and keep them continually laughing made him an expert at what the magicians call "presentation," which involves a similar kind of semihypnotic skill.

It was only after I had gradually got to know him that we talked about literature and religion. In the meantime, I had been rather astonished by the success of his second novel, *The Last Hurrah*, which was not only so much more successful commercially than *The Oracle* had been but was also quite three-dimensional as the earlier book was not. Ed O'Connor became not only rich but a writer to be specially noted—though his financial success was at once so conspicuous that the reviewers, in this case and in the cases of his subsequent novels, were unwilling to acknowledge this. What with a prize, a movie contract, and a large advance from his publisher, *The Last Hurrah* had made many thousands of dollars before a word of it had been printed; and, with the exception of the unsatisfactory interludes of the diabolic fairy tale *Benjy* and the adapted play *I Was Dancing*, his later books were also best-sellers. These, *The Edge of Sadness* and *All in the Family*, were occupied, like *The Last Hurrah*, with the Irish Catholic world of Boston, which had never before been exploited with this seriousness, intelligence, and intimate knowledge. *The Last Hurrah* had dealt with the old-fashioned Irish political boss, frankly corrupt and feudally benevolent; *The Edge of Sadness* dealt with the priesthood and, in one of its most effective scenes, pitted the sophisticated and snobbish Boston priest against the sincere ascetic who has chosen to mortify himself by devotion to an illiterate and discouraging parish; his last novel, *All in the Family,* represents the Kennedy generation which stands somewhere between the old Irish world of Boston and the new world of cocktails and enlightenment. In all this, there is no attempt whatever to fall into the once-accepted clichés and represent the Irish Americans as lovable or humorously happy-go-lucky or, except in a satiric fashion, to touch the chords of "Mother Machree." O'Connor gives us rather the brutal and quarrelsome and histrionic sides of the Irish, and his attitude toward them, though friendly, is sometimes extremely acid. He specialized in hypocritical, tyrannical, and completely self-centered old men—old Carmody in *The Edge of Sadness,* who exhibits a scene of contrition on what is supposed to be his deathbed, but repudiates it when he recovers—and vituperative and wrangling old women, such as the sister in *I Was Dancing.* He composed so many conversations in which the parties were slanging and scoring off one another that I was interested to hear him say, after his first visit to Ireland, that he could not stand the literary life of the pubs—Ed did not drink at all—on account of its malignant backbiting. I was amused by his relations with Mayor Curley, who had more or less inspired Frank Skeffington, the boss politician of *The Last Hurrah.* A Boston paper sent the book to Curley, inviting him to review it. Curley looked at it and wrote the editor that he was putting the matter in the hands of his lawyer. When, however, the author by chance met the mayor for the first time, the latter said, "What I liked best was where I say on my deathbed that if I had my life over, I'd do it all over again." It was *The Last Hurrah,* apparently, that stimulated Curley later to write an account of his life. He there confessed to misdeeds that profoundly shocked Ed: Ed could never have invented such unscrupulous wicked- ness as Curley's public support of the Ku Klux Klan, let alone a public official who was shameless enough to tell about them.

Yet Ed's powers of invention were of the vital kind that not merely reports on a social group but that produces imaginary personalities. Though, for example, he knew the Kennedys and was very much interested in watching their careers, the Kinsellas of *All in the Family* are some- thing quite other than the Kennedys. But curiosity about the Kennedys gave rise, for the book, to a false publicity —which Ed did nothing to encourage—as a kind of *roman à clef*. Aside from the fact that the younger Kin sellas—the family in the novel—are of the Ivy League generation of Boston Irish, I cannot see that the dramatic situations to which their respective careers gave rise have much in common with the adventures of the Kennedys. They took place entirely in the imagined world which Edwin O'Connor had created. So I found out in talking to Ed that the ecumenical priest in the Kinsella family who is always going away on missions to non-Catholic churches and of whom it is said that in his present phase he will hardly speak to a Catholic is as much a comic invention as the manager of the Dublin hotel with his ironical glamorizing of Ireland and his curious unexpected laugh. Ed was also a master of mimicry, in dramatizing his anecdotes in conversation as well as in making his creations talk. Certain of his friends and acquaintances became his favorite evocations, whom he was able to imitate so vividly that they almost became characters in his fiction. The two phonograph readings which he made from his novels show that in this capacity he might have qualified as a professional entertainer. He was very atten- tive to accents, and it is interesting on these records to hear the voices in which he imagined Skeffington and his other characters speaking. His one dramatic weakness, which he was trying to overcome, was his tendency to prolong conversations, making them loop around and around without satisfactorily progressing. This, I think, was his chief difficulty in writing plays, in which a dialogue must not go on too long and must take steps to arrive at some destination.

In the meantime, the effect on Ed of passing suddenly from the routine of radio to riches and reputation was to make him play a new role of humorous ostentation. I think, however, that he perhaps really reveled in his passing to this luxury from his old habitation. I remember his saying on one occasion that he had to go back to Boston in order to be "near the bank." He purchased a Mercedes, which he treasured with special solicitude, and he rented —at, I learn, however, a very low rate, since the owner was an enthusiastic admirer—a magnificent residence on Chestnut Street, the property of a rich Boston art lover who had furnished it with Renaissance Italian furniture and other foreign rarities in the taste of Isabella Gardner's museum in Boston. There was a sedan chair in the hall, and I told him that I supposed he used it to be carried up to the State House every day—an idea which he at once accepted. This establishment reminded me of a story that a friend of mine had told me of having once had dinner in Boston at the house of "Honey Fitz," a prominent local politician. There had been footmen who waited on table in knee breeches and silk stockings. Fitzgerald called one of them over for the benefit of the guest. "See," he said, pinching the footman's calf, "two pairs." "Why two pairs?" "He's a hairy son of a bitch!" Ed enjoyed playing some such role, and I never could be sure, when I visited him, that we were not in one of his novels. He developed a slight impatience of a kind characteristic of the rich with the tiresome, the incompetent and the undependable. He later moved into and actually purchased an even more monstrous mansion on Marlboro Street just off Arlington which he said the former owner had built with the ambition of being the possessor of the biggest private house in Boston. When we first went to dinner there, Ed said, as he showed us in—referring to the mansion itself—"We have to go through this gate house first." It was a little too large for comfort. The rooms were too spacious to talk across, and one would have to group in isolated pairs that were out of communication with one another. Along the wall, beneath the high ceilings, were empty niches that should have had busts in them. It proved, however, to be too much for the O'Connors to keep up, and Ed eventually sold it at a profit.

This was not the literary life as the New York intellectuals understood it. Ed's two later novels were also best-sellers, and a literary intellectual objects to nothing so much as a best-selling book that also possesses real merit. Only Irish Catholic readers, who recognized, as one of them told me, all their "old uncles and aunts" in these books, seem fully to have appreciated them, and, except for Mr. John V. Kelleher, in an article in *The Atlantic*, no one, so far as I know, wrote anything intelligent about them. Yet *The Edge of Sadness* and *All in the Family* went much deeper than *The Last Hurrah*. They are only incidentally humorous. In the first of these, the dreariness, the blankness, of the priest's lonely Christmas in his decaying parish represents the ordeal and the unrewarded triumph of Father Kennedy's religious vocation. I was unaware until Ed told me that Father Kennedy's dedication to this unattractive and alien neighborhood, inhabited mostly by Syrians, Greeks, Italians, "a few Chinese," and "the advance guard of Puerto Ricans," assisted by his boring and ridiculous Polish curate, who, however, is given his moments of dignity, represented an attempt on the part of the author to encourage the Catholic Church in Boston to work beyond the somewhat exclusive limits which the Irish had tended to impose on it. In his next novel, *All in the Family,* he is evidently trying to deal, in a firm although underground way, with the sexual puritanism of Irish Catholicism. The unexplained suicide of the narrator's mother is echoed and balanced later on by the unfaithfulness and flight of his wife—which, however, since times are changing, does not turn out to be equally serious, for the couple are later reunited. At the time of Ed's death, he had begun a new novel about an eighty-year-old cardinal—the inevitable O'Connor old man!—who knows that he is doomed to die of cancer. At his age and trained in the traditional ways, he cannot understand what at the present time is going on in the Catholic Church, and Mr. Kelleher tells us that he was to be confronted with a variety of Catholic types who would give voice to a variety of points of view.

At some point, when I was spending my winters in Cambridge, Ed and I decided to compose together, contributing alternate chapters, a novel about a magician named Baldini. The results of this kind of collaboration may turn out to be very curious. In 1907, at William Dean Howells's suggestion, the editor of *Harper's Bazar* published a serial called *The Whole Family,* of which each chapter, supposed to be written by a different member of the family, was contributed by a different American novelist. "The Married Son," who is an artist and hopes to study in France, was assigned to Henry James, who developed it with his usual patience and scrupulously prepared a confrontation which was to lead up to the chapter that was to follow; but it evidently did not occur to him that there would be nobody, according to the scheme of the story, to report, except at secondhand, what happened in this private interview on a bench in Central Park, and Elizabeth Stuart Phelps, a writer of religious novels, who was to do "The Married Daughter" chapter, disregarded this proffered cue and went on with no reference to what had gone before to rather a vulgar un-Jamesian monologue. So, in writing alternate chapters with Ed, I very soon ran into difficulties. He would not always accept my cues or my methods, and I found my narrative blocked. I suspected that this was deliberate and that we were playing a game of chess, and this suspicion has been corroborated by Mrs. O'Connor's telling me that, in sending back Chapter 4, Ed had said to her with satisfaction, "Well, I guess I've got him now." One of our principal points of divergence was that I wanted to keep the conjuring within the limits of the possible, whereas Ed did not hesitate to make it fantastic. The trick, for example, of the chosen card that appears between two plates of glass is something every conjuror knows, but it was plausible that Baldini at that time should not yet know that it had been found to be possible to set the trick off through an electronic device, by simply raising one's voice at a distance from the frame. Then the elephant: it was true that Houdini had been able to make an elephant disappear on the ample Hippodrome stage which had room for a very large cabinet in which the vanishing elephant could be concealed. But Ed wanted to have Baldini perform the trick out-of-doors in the Yankee Stadium "beneath the folds of crimson and gold" of an all-enfolding wrap, as is possible with the levitated girl who, covered with a similar blanket, has been floated out over the audience and then, when the blanket has been snatched away, is seen to have disappeared. I had to accept this, although I could not imagine the practical means by which the feat could be accomplished. Another thing that

annoyed me though I had to accept it, too, was the appearance of Derek Marchmont. I had invented him merely in
order to introduce his complaint, on the grounds of good
taste, of the practice of an American magician of producing a borrowed pearl necklace from his mouth which
I had seen in the London Letter of the magician's magazine *The Sphinx*. I had not been prepared to have Ed
bring him back in the role of an important character. We
thus very soon reached an impasse, and having then other
things to do, I dropped *Baldini* for two years or so. I was
planning, however, to revive it, not wanting to be out-
witted by Ed, and, not very long before his death, had not
the manuscript out to study it. I shall not discuss my
further plans for it till I have presented the unfinished
fragment itself.

# *Baldini*

## *Chapter 1*

### (E.W.)

Jack Baldini was baffled.

He had seen the trick a hundred times: the chosen card with the corner torn off that suddenly appeared in the frame between the two panes of glass. But in Esmeralda's apartment there was no confederate to set it off, at least none that Baldini could see, nor could he detect any threads. She had simply taken the frame from a shelf and set it up on the table.

"A camera timer?" he asked.

"Guess again." She let him wonder a moment. "No, a new electronics job. Cute? All I have to do is raise my voice. Or a pistol shot if you want that old gag."

Without giving him a chance to examine it, she put the apparatus away.

"That's one I hadn't heard about," he was forced to admit. "It might open up huge horizons."

"It's not on the market," she said, pouring him another drink from the cloisonné cocktail shaker.

She offered him a stuffed date.

"Do they go with absinthe?"

"I love them."

He stood up, with the date in his fingers, and looked about her curious living room. He was embarrassed at her scoring off him with the new electronics trick.

"You've got some nice items here."

There were photographs of Adelaide Hermann and other woman magicians, besides several of Esmeralda— Esmeralda the Great, as she called herself, one showing her in the toreador costume in which she always opened her show. To the accompaniment of fiery music, she would maneuver with a bullfighter's cape and produce from it a bouquet of silk flowers, a pair of red rubber lobsters, a bowl of goldfish, a bird cage with a plastic parakeet, and finally a pretty Spanish dancer, who carried on with the castanets while Esmeralda changed to something more feminine: a simple green evening gown, which seemed to offer no place of concealment for the properties that magicians call "loads."

One picture Jack Baldini did not like to see: a signed photograph of handsome Derek Marchmont, the distinguished English magician, in his flight commander's uniform embellished with decorations. He had a BBC voice and accent which Baldini could not abide, and at the time when he had contributed a London column to an American magicians' magazine, he had complained of the bad taste of an American performer, who had borrowed a lady's necklace, pretended to spill the pearls in an omelet, tasted a morsel of the omelet and then produced the necklace intact from his mouth. He had now returned to London after a highly successful visit to the States, during which he had appeared with Danny Kaye: but there had been a good deal of talk about him and Esmeralda, and now Baldini thought he noticed a distinct veneer of BBC overlaying Esmeralda's Middle Western accent. And her father was a circus man! He found the stuffed date rather sickening.

"But that's gimmicks, that electronic card-frame!" He turned abruptly and addressed her with a loud authority. *"You* don't need gimmicks, Mamie! There's nobody that doesn't need gimmicks like you. Won't you show me that dice routine, darling, that everybody raves about. I've only heard about it—I've never seen you do it."

"Oh, that silly old routine," she replied. "You really want to see it?"

"I'm crazy to."

She left the room. Jack resented as unbecoming what he felt was a false note of modesty that she had learned no doubt from the gentlemanly Marchmont.

He studied, where it stood in a corner, made uncanny by a mask-shaded light, a replica of the Iron Maiden of Nuremberg, which he had never seen her use on the stage and which seemed to him a little more sinister than anything he would care to use himself.

She came back with two very large dice boxes, from which she scattered on the table large dice. Then with brusque and rapid gestures, as if with impatience, she shuffled them about on the table with the dice boxes held bottom up. He admired her long expert fingers. She seemed to be shoving the dice off the table, but when one looked at the carpet, they were not there, and then, when she lifted up the boxes, they would be seen to be piled up neatly in stacks as if they were children's blocks. Later on, they all seemed to coagulate to produce two larger dice, and then these coalesced in one giant. This was a magician's trick, which required enormous skill, but—since it could not be watched on a stage—was quite useless for public performance.

"Mamie, you're out of this world!" exclaimed Jack. He took a sip of his absinthe cocktail in its queerly calyxed, green-glass goblet. He thought he knew where the dice had gone, but he refrained from scrutinizing her bodice, whose contents so invited admiration. Or *did* he know? He usually could see what his masculine confreres were up to. But did she hypnotize him, or was it the absinthe that left him somewhat puzzled and dazed? He found that he was suddenly shy about bringing up the business he had come to discuss. He had to pluck up his courage. She was a master magician undoubtedly, but then, after all, so was he. They both stood at the top of their profession, and there had come to be between them a certain rivalry. But why should they not join their forces? Why not do a show together? The element of the dramatic and the picturesque was something they had always had in common. Their shows were both brilliant masquerades. Not only did Esmeralda open with her toreador "production" act, she appeared again in Spanish costume at the end of the first half of the show and sang a flamenco, which ended with a flight of tumbler pigeons (instead of the conventional doves), released from a small casket, which, as she sang, contained her true love's heart; and then later, yet again as a Castilian beauty, when she would "vanish," in magic parlance, a lover whom she had hidden behind a screen, simultaneously with a frantic husband who had rushed behind the screen to kill him: a shot was heard, and then the screen was folded up and removed—both the men had disappeared. As for Jack, he did impersonations and, as was recognized, delightful ones: an Italian, a Chinaman, an Austrian, all imitated from foreign magicians—his bald head made wig-wearing easy; and in one of his "illusions" he sprang into a chest as a hunted Sicilian gangster, and then when the chest was shown empty, he suddenly appeared in a box, wearing kilts and a Harry Lauder cap and shouting, "Hoots, Jack Baldini, laddie, 'tis a bonnie braw act ye gie us!" and vaulted down onto the stage, to be met by tremendous applause. And Esmeralda had long exercised on Jack a

queer kind of fascination; he had seen her show again
and again. Though they had always been on friendly
terms, she had held him off, he felt, as a male competitor,
and he wanted to know her better. After years of cute
little assistants, who had been chosen for their appearance
in short skirts, high heels, and bras, as well as for some
modest competence as contortionists or acrobats which
qualified them to turn cartwheels at the end of an act and
to compress themselves into narrow spaces for the girl
who is sawed in two or the girl in the wicker basket
which is run through and through with swords, he felt
that he could love such a woman. Did he love her already? He hardly dared ask. With her rich and abundant
black hair, her long artificial lashes, her full figure, and
her mesmeric gaze which made "false direction" so easy
that, for her fellow magicians, no matter how persuasive,
it almost appeared to be cheating, she seemed sometimes
a real enchantress who possessed some power other than
that of trickery when she would cause a great iridescent
ball to float out over the heads of the audience or produce
at command from an aluminum shaker which had previously been shown to be empty innumerable kinds of
drinks. One did know how these tricks were done, but
there were others of which she had never told the secret
and which none of her fellow magicians could do. Jack
had realized, since looking at that photograph of the so
much admired Marchmont, that he could not introduce
into his own new show a burlesque of a British magician.

But he now decided to take the leap. "Mamie," he began, "you and I have the only shows in magic now that
are really imaginative works of art, the only shows with
real personality—"

She forestalled him before he had finished: "I'm glad
you came in tonight, Jack. I've been toying with the notion of a project that I think you might possibly be in-

terested in. Since Derek's gone back to England, I don't know anybody else I could trust."

"What is it?"

She looked at the grandfather's clock, which was one of the guaranteed American antiques that contrasted so oddly with her more exotic furnishings.

"There isn't time for it now, I'm afaid. I'll have to dash out in a minute. I've got to be in a benefit tonight, and I've got to get to the goddam hall to check on my props and things."

Since it was Sunday, he had hoped to have dinner with her.

"What benefit?"

"The crippled glassblowers."

This was puzzling, but he did not inquire.

"Can't you give me some idea what you have in mind?"

"I'd rather talk about it when we've got more time. Come around after the show on Thursday."

"I've had an idea, too. A kind of a dramatic show that we might do together—"

"You won't need your accents and false mustaches for the act that I'm thinking about."

He felt a little hurt.

"My public are used to seeing me in character—"

"After a minute or two, you won't be seen at all," she said. She grinned in the friendly way that always made her audiences feel that the sorceress was one of themselves —the women that she was one of the girls, the men that they could take her out.

She struck a Javanese bell with her palm, and the girl who played the Spanish dancer came in, without looking at Jack.

"Get the floating globe ready." And to Jack: "Have you seen my new one? I've got the whole geography of the world on it. It lights up from inside and looks lovely.

When it's hanging in the middle of the house, it explodes and scares them crazy. It's a poor night when we don't get some screams. I can't do all that, though, this evening— Well, goodbye now. See you Thursday."

She held out her sharp-nailed hand. Not so practical for card work, he thought. Except of course for marking the backs.


## Chapter 2

### (E.O'C.)


Baldini lived in a small apartment on the West Side, an apartment so small that, had it not been for the magician's cunning, it would have seemed barely habitable. Thanks, however, to a most ingenious arrangement of mirrors, the place looked easily seven times its size, and the casual visitor, entering Baldini's tiny—nine by twelve—drawing room for the first time, received instantly the impression of limitless space.

For three days following his Sunday meeting with Esmeralda, Baldini remained in his apartment. There was work to do, he did not do it. More than a month before, he had agreed to perform his wonders at a children's party, to be given by the irascible soda-crackers monopolist, Shepherd O'Brien. Moreover, in a moment of weakness, he had agreed to perform his most celebrated illusion— the Vanishing Elephant. The party was to have been on Monday. Monday came, the children gathered, the air rang with shrill voices and the crunching of a million soda crackers, but—Baldini was not there.

He had stayed at home. For the first time in his professional career, the conjurer had failed to fulfill an engagement. For a time he attempted to justify his behavior to himself by complaining of the lack of props. Elephants, he reminded himself, were in notoriously short supply these days; then too, once secured, they were apt to be something of a nuisance offstage. Expensive, too; Baldini was not cheap, but the thought of his bills for hay alone sometimes made him shudder.

Still, the trick was a great one. The effect of a mature elephant, vanishing at a word from beneath the folds of crimson and gold with which the magician had draped it —this was something to behold! Baldini knew this, it was the trick of which he was most proud; it was the trick which, above all others, had gained him his enviable reputation—and yet it was a trick for which he now felt something very close to hatred! For it was this trick—this same superb illusion—which had once made him a figure of fun in the eyes of Esmeralda.

It had happened nearly a year ago now. He had promised to perform the feat for her alone; he had chosen as his site a deserted corner beneath the center-field bleachers at Yankee Stadium. He had performed as never before; even the fact that Esmeralda had appeared accompanied by Derek Marchmont had failed to dim the luster of his performance. The silken folds swiftly and silently cloaked Randy, the doubletusked behemoth, and then, at the single peremptory magical word *"Neh-ru!"*, the silk was whisked away and the great beast was gone!

Esmeralda's eyes had shone, her lovely, luscious body had quivered with an admiration which was close to passion, it was a moment for which Jack Baldini had hoped for years. But alas, it was a moment which was destined to be spoiled. For Derek Marchmont, consumed with envy, nevertheless had leaned negligently on his whangee and said, in a drawling voice, "Good show, Sabu!"

*Sabu!* With the utterance of the dreadful word, so humiliating in its implications, a change had come over Esmeralda's face. On her full lips suddenly appeared the

slightest of smiles, a mocking light came into her eyes,
and Baldini, with sinking heart, knew that he was forever
to be joined in unlovely combine with a dwarfish, nut-
brown mahout.

From that awful day, he had eliminated the Elephant
Vanish from his repertoire. It had made a difference,
even to an illusionist of Baldini's astonishing versatility;
the old proverb "To lose an elephant is to make a hole"
has seldom found truer illustration. Yet such was the
measure of his skill that he had been able to survive the
calamity; his gifts for mimicry and disguise had stood him
in good stead. Joining them to his magnificent technical
abilities, he had remained at the top of his profession,
and only Baldini himself knew how bitterly he mourned
the loss of his *pièce de résistance,* and how eagerly, how
passionately he had planned for some trick, a great trick,
a *Baldini* trick: a trick worthy of succeeding its splendid
predecessor.

And now, at last, he had found it! A trick so astonishing, so ingenious, so induplicable that, once performed, it
would be his forever. His—and Esmeralda's. For in the
performance of this simple yet extravagant illusion he
would require a confederate. And no ordinary confederate
—in a word, no "stooge"—would do. No, here he needed
someone who commanded a powerful stage presence,
who was at home in the great, rather than the routine,
feats of magic, and who was, above all else, a *woman.*

Esmeralda, of course, who else? No one; among the
prestidigitators of her sex, it was Esmeralda who stood
paramount. He was eager to confide in her, to tell her at
once every last detail of his scheme for their joint future,
yet here he was, alone in his apartment, forced to wait
until the appointed Thursday. It was a necessity which
left him impatient, even mildly angry; with a frown he
filled his sword-stick with absinthe and slowly began to
drink from it. Glasses, goblets, and tumblers were all very

well in their way, but when it came to serious drinking, Baldini had always felt there was nothing like a sword-stick.

After about a half hour of steady drinking, Baldini rose from his chair and began to perform. Drink, he knew, had a retarding effect on other magicians; on him, however, its only effect was to sharpen his wits. Watching himself covertly in the multiple mirrors in which his apartment abounded, it seemed to Baldini that he had never been more brilliant. Cards poured from his hands in bewildering profusion, often, in midair, apparently changing in color and size; a live rabbit was produced, not from a hat, but from an object no larger than a tennis ball; then, turning to his genius for impersonation, he mimicked the great Chinese magician Long Tack San in his most renowned trick: placing a bowl of water in his hands, he completed a somersault in the air, emerging with the bowl still full and, moreover, three goldfish swimming about. Baldini, as he did this trick, became completely submerged in the character of the agile Chinese; rather short and portly himself, he seemed to gain at least a foot in height, and his eyes acquired a peculiar slant; most astonishing of all was the fact that, although he was bald as an egg, he now, without recourse to a wig of any sort, seemed possessed of a full head of lank black hair!

He rounded out his performance by doing a short but debasing imitation of Derek Marchmont. He did a series of easy, almost childishly simple tricks, and did them clumsily. As he performed, he talked. In the beginning, Derek's BBC accent was faithfully duplicated; then, as cards slipped from his fingers, as props fell to the floor, as effect after effect of the supercilious Britisher failed to come off, Baldini altered his voice so that eventually it became a revolting, supplicating cockney whine.

"Lor' lumme, Guv'nor!" wheedled the pseudo-Marchmont. "I ain't 'arf bad todye, I ain't! 'Arf a mo' wile I give it anuvver try!"

This pleased Baldini; as the sword-stick tilted once more to his lips, he smiled thinly and thought of the possibility of actually reducing his rival to such abjection. Perhaps when he and Esmeralda had presented their act, he could somehow bring this to pass.

Meanwhile, on Thursday, there was Esmeralda. He would, at that time, inform her of his plans. And it was only now, for the first time, that he recalled her saying that *she* had some plans! Plans that, apparently, included both of them, plans that might very well parallel his own. For she had spoken, in a casual way, of the possibility of their appearing together: this was all to the good. What was *not* all to the good was the suggestion that in this act Baldini would be both silent and invisible. It was not quite what he had in mind for himself; shrewd showman that he was, he felt instinctively that if he could neither be seen nor heard, his role might perhaps be a subordinate one.

Was this, in fact, what Esmeralda really wanted? Could this be? Was it perhaps conceivable that the whole proposal had been cunningly inspired by the distant Marchmont? Baldini frowned and went once more to his sword-stick. He simply did not know; he would have to wait until Thursday to find out.

### Chapter 3

#### (E.W.)

"You were terrific, darling," said Jack, when he found Esmeralda in her dressing room after her show on Thursday night. "What gets me is that you didn't just clip those pigeons so they wouldn't get away. You taught them that circus routine so that they fly around the house and then come and perch on your shoulders."

"Oh, I hoped you'd miss that silly production act. Production is such a bore. I've put in some gags to make it even sillier so people will begin to laugh: the sausages and the cabbages and the lobsters. I've been playing with the idea of a chamberpot. Let it slop out and then pretend to empty it on the audience." She made a brusque gesture of flinging the contents.

"I don't like it. I'd cut all that out. It's beneath the dignity of a show like yours. Just build up the pigeons and the dancer. Maybe a big silk with a bull's head. That thing that you wave around suddenly turns out to have a bull on it."

"I'd like to have a real bull, but they're not as easy to handle as elephants."

He was silent a moment. Was this a sneer?

"Have a bull with a man inside, if you really want to be that comic. Then Irena could dance with the bull."

"Irena isn't a comic. She wants to be taken as a serious artist. I wanted her to skip rope with the sausages and it made her furious."

"What about your floating ball? It didn't explode to-night."

"I haven't got it rigged right yet, and I didn't want to spoil the act."

"Sardi's restaurant," said Baldini to the taxi driver.

"Let's go where we can be more private." She gave the man another address.

It was a dark little restaurant in the West Fifties where Jack had never been before. She led him to a corner table.

"Let me hear *your* idea first," he said, when they had ordered spiced-beef sandwiches and Pernods.

She demurred for a moment, reflected. "If you've got something to say, say it now."

He needed the support of the Pernod, and he drank it
all down in two draughts.

"It's this idea I've had for a show. Now, you're the
biggest woman magician that the world has seen since
Adelaide Hermann."

"She wasn't so hot," said Esmeralda, chewing a bite
from the sandwich. "She just used Hermann's old illusions after his death."

"All right then—there never was a woman magician
who was in the same class as you—and very few men, I
may add." As she stared at him, not recognizing a com-
pliment, he was sorry he had added this. "Well, there've
never in the history of magic been two top-flight magicians who worked together—a man and woman would
make it sensational. I've been thinking that you and I
could put on a show that would mark a new summit in
magic."

He paused. She was attentive, perhaps interested.

"Of course, you'd have some wonderful ideas, and I've
got a few myself. Here's my conception of the second
half. The Queen of Sheba comes to see Solomon. She
comes in on a richly caparisoned elephant with a body-
guard in beautiful costumes and ladies of the court and
all that. Solomon bows low and greets her in a guttural
ancient Hebrew accent—he speaks like old Schildkraut
when he was playing in English. Long handsome beard
and scepter and a huge high crown on his head. She
smiles at him graciously and proudly dismounts. Solomon
flourishes his scepter, and the elephant disappears. My
old gag, but it'll do to start with," he added in a depreca-
tory tone. "Waiter, two more of these—Well, Solomon
and Sheba are both magicians, and they vie with one another giving presents and performing miracles. He gives
her a big bowl of goldfish—we'd have to have it made a
special shape so it wouldn't look too much like a party for

the kiddies—and she whips out a purple silk shawl with the Star of David on it. He comes back with an ostrich-feather headdress, and she counters with a couple of dwarfs that play leapfrog and turn handsprings. He lets fly with the tumbler pigeons that go to perch on her shoulders. Then Solomon claps his hands, and a banquet appears from nowhere—the attendants all have flowing robes. Sheba takes a jug from one of her maidens and asks Solomon what he'll have to drink: white wine or red wine or mead or myrrh or whatever they drank in those days. He says he'll have a highball—that brings a laugh— and she pours out a mahogany-colored number. She says she always starts with Pernod, and she pours out some-thing cloudy. Then comes the sauterne and Burgundy, and she asks the major-domo what he'll have. He says a Bloody Mary. Solomon raises his eyebrows. 'You must have been out with the Golden Calf,' he says. Then what will her chief lady-in-waiting have? 'A very dry martini, please, Your Highness.' 'Olive or onion?' she asks. 'She was out last night, too,' she says to Solomon, 'but Char-mian's a girl who can take it.' Of course we'll do better than this—I'm just improvising at the moment. While they're dining, the dancing girls dance—that gives Irena a chance for her act—and when the banquet is over, the major-domo pulls the cloth away from under the things on the table and begins to juggle with the cups and plates. I've got a topnotch juggler, and he can sail plates out over the audience. What happens at the end we'd have to decide. I've got one new stunt that I'd like to have you see."

She had listened without interrupting, smoking her cigarette. Yet he felt that he had not succeeded in com-municating to her his own enthusiasm. But now she said, "Maybe I've got it," looking down and flicking the ash.

He was taken aback for a moment: his heart had been set on the trick on which he had been working so passionately, but after all they might use them both. "What do you have in mind?" he asked.

"Well, you know the old challenging problem that nobody has ever solved: how to make a man disappear, without any drops or traps, in full view of the audience."

"It could be done with mirrors but hard to manage."

"Mirrors are out," she said. "How do you get him behind them without having something to hide it—and then, anything that's near enough is going to be reflected in the mirrors."

"My juggler might distract attention."

"I think I've got the solution."

"She vanishes the major-domo." He was fitting it into the spectacle.

"I need a good magician. It would have to be you."

"And then Solomon appears in a box, and he makes a majestic bow like Chaliapin in *Boris Godunov*." Demonstrating, he bowed from the waist and, trailing his right arm, saluted from the level of his cheek.

She did not comment.

"Well, what's the gimmick?" He gave her the smile of a man of the world.

"I haven't got it all worked out yet. It's a little bit tricky—I've been getting into things that you can't always depend on for a public performance. Let's talk about it later."

"But you think that our show's a good notion?"

"Let's think about it. I'll call you up."

"Well, let me tell you the idea *I've* been working on."

"I've got to get home," she said. "Irena's got some kind of bug, and I sent her home to bed after the opening act. You tell me about it next time."

He concealed his disappointment and paid the check.

"Why the glassblowers?" he asked, as they were going out.

"That benefit? Oh, I'm crazy about them. It fascinates

me to see them do it—making vases and goblets and things. And I like to see them swell and swell and then go off."

"The glass, you mean?"

"Yes, they blow those big glass bubbles, and if they keep on blowing, the bubble explodes. I used to know a professional glassblower, and I used to make him do it for me."

"He was the only man you ever loved," said Baldini on a tone of banter.

"I had a passion for him," she said, "while he lasted. It makes some people nervous to watch it." She laughed. "And if the pieces fall on you, they burn—it's molten."

Baldini was silent.

"Don't take me home," she said.

"Of course I'll take you home— We might have that in the show," he said, as they were sitting in the taxi. "It's another of Sheba's entertainments. There's your perfect distraction. The glassblower makes vases for Solomon, and then when one explodes, he vanishes."

"I'm working on it, but you have to have a furnace and a lot of apparatus."

She smiled warmly when he dropped her at her door, with a caress of her velvet eyes.

"I'll hear from you?—I can get the backing."

It was too early to kiss her, he thought.

Ah, what a queen she would make, riding in on his well-trained elephant!

## Chapter 4

### (E.O'C.)

There followed two weeks in which Baldini did not see Esmeralda. He talked to her once over the telephone; she had called him to cancel a dinner date. It was during this call she had announced, disquietingly, that she had had second thoughts about "Solomon and Sheba"; she was now against it. Furious, he had asked why.

"Physically, Sheba's not right for me," she said. "With that long nose and everything."

As patiently as he could, he explained to her that she was thinking not of Sheba but of Cleopatra.

"Oh, well," she said negligently, "what's the difference?"

It was a maddening question. Baldini was not an intellectual snob, but he had majored in history at Long Island University. Only the fact of Esmeralda's beauty saved her from a cutting and well-merited rebuke.

And yet he was not as upset about this as he would have been a week ago. The simple truth was that the "Solomon and Sheba" routine had begun to seem less attractive to him—considerably less attractive. He was unwilling, as he grew older, to work his old Elephant Vanish. Not merely because Derek Marchmont had once poked fun at this feat; not merely because there was some slight element of danger to his person; but more because with age his skill increased, and he had now reached the point where he feared that one day he would perform so skillfully that the elephant would indeed vanish in fact, instead of simply *appearing* to do so. And if *this* should happen—if, thanks to his magic, the elephant *really* disappeared and could not be returned—it would mean that he would lose a fresh elephant with every performance! Baldini was not without private means, but he was reasonably certain that such an expense would soon prove burdensome.

He went back, now, to some of his old tricks that he had experimented with years ago, but had abandoned. Levitation in particular captured his attention once again. He envisioned Esmeralda, placed in a handsome mother-of-pearl sarcophagus, drifting slowly over the heads of the audience—could this be done? He thought it could, and if so, it would be a far more effective trick than her own proposed feat of vanishing a man or woman without the use of drops or drapes. Indeed, as a showman, he had a certain contempt for this trick; privately he thought it good enough for a woman magician, but not quite up to the standard he had established for himself.

He called Esmeralda at the end of two weeks.

"Mamie: tomorrow at eight?"

She had agreed—it seemed to him reluctantly.

"Is it terribly important?" she said. "I'm really not in very good shape."

"Your shape always looks good to me," he sniggered. As soon as he said this, he knew he had done it again. It was his weakness: the coarse streak which occasionally cracked through his otherwise impeccable veneer. He suspected that in the past it had cost him employment at several children's parties.

"Good night," she said icily. Though of Hungarian birth, she was always the perfect lady.

The following evening, Baldini took a taxi to Esmeralda's apartment house. As usual, he proposed to the driver that they toss for the fare: double or nothing; as usual, the driver accepted; as usual, thanks to his manipulative skill, Baldini paid nothing. It was a way he had of cutting down expenses.

He went up to her apartment quickly, and a little nervously. Would she be angry still, following his coarseness of the evening before? He hoped not, but if she were, he was confident that what he had to tell her would melt her wrath.

To his surprise, he heard voices, laughter through her door. He pushed the buzzer; there was a silence, then the sound of scuffing, then, finally, the door opened and there stood Esmeralda, her eyes shining, a glass in her hand.

"Why, Jack!" she said. "That's right, you were coming tonight, weren't you?"

He nodded; he did not trust himself to speak.

"Well, come in, come in," she cried. Possibly because she was a European, she added, *"Entrez!"* Her hand shot out in a beckoning gesture; from her fingers seemed to flow a succession of gay, multicolored silk flags.

What a ham, thought Baldini morosely: always on stage. And with those lousy, childish tricks! But he went in, and as he crossed the threshold, he stopped short. For there, lounging negligently on the long expensive couch that he—Baldini—had given Esmeralda for her birthday, was Derek Marchmont!

"Hello, Goldoni," he drawled. "Long time no see!"

Goldoni! It was the last straw! Baldini boiled with rage, he wanted more than anything else in the world to reach out, grab this insolent British mountebank, and beat him into insensibility. Unfortunately, he could not do this. His innate good manners forbade it; also the knowledge that he would receive a severe trouncing.

He stood there, seething quietly. Marchmont rose languidly from the couch, unexpectedly performed a front somersault, and came up smiling and bearing in his hands a small fish bowl, filled to the brim, and with a single goldfish swimming around in it.

"My compliments," he said mockingly, handing the bowl to Baldini. "Think of it as a tranquilizer, old man; it will help you while you seethe."

"Now, now, boys," said Esmeralda prettily. "Let's all be friends and have a party. After all, Jack, Derek's just flown over from England. He's only been here a few days."

"I didn't expect to be here at all, actually," drawled Marchmont. "But duty called: I had to give a command performance at the glassblowers' benefit."

Baldini stared at Esmeralda. "The glassblowers' benefit? But that's the one *you* were—"

She cut in smoothly; too smoothly, he thought. "Imagine my surprise," she said, "to find Derek on the bill with me. And all the time I thought he was in England!"

"England couldn't contain me, dear lady," said Derek, with a flourish, "as long as you and the glassblowers were here!"

If it weren't for my rage, thought Baldini, I would be nauseated. Fighting a desire to drown them both in a cascade of vituperation, he said, as calmly as he could, "I see. You performed together, then?"

"Quite," said Marchmont. "And brilliantly, may I add. Not a rehearsal, everything improvised, yet it all went like clockwork. Even Esmeralda's pigeons seemed to take to me; it was as if we'd worked together for years!"

"Yes, it was lovely," Esmeralda said, and Baldini noticed that a glow came into her eyes as she said this. He felt like running her through with his sword-stick. Continuing, she said animatedly, "In fact, Jack, Derek and I have something to tell you!"

"I wonder if you can guess what it is?" asked Marchmont nastily. "Eh, Goldoni? You should be able to, you know: a man with your professional background. Didn't you once do a mind-reading act? Extrasensory perception and all that sort of thing? Well, think hard, old man, and see if the master mentalist can't put two and two together and come up with four. Look here, I'll even give you a clue!"

And with just the trace of a sneer on his thin aristocratic lips, Marchmont began to juggle a series of thin golden bands, finger-size, in the air; at the same time he hummed nasally a tune which Baldini, after a moment or two, recognized as "The Wedding March." He stared, first at Marchmont, then at Esmeralda, with horrified eyes; thanks to his training as a master mentalist, he was beginning to glimpse just what the despised Marchmont was driving at.

"Get it, old man?" said Marchmont, smirking unpleasantly. "Not too subtle for you?"

"Oh Derek, you're such a clown!" cried Esmeralda, giggling happily.

It was the first time Baldini had ever heard Esmeralda giggle; it struck him as a most unbecoming sound. It was the last sound he heard before slumping to the floor. Jack Baldini had fainted.

I must not finish the story along my own lines now that Ed cannot contribute his chapters, but I shall give a brief summary of what I intended.

My next chapter was to take place in a New York shop that dealt in magic supplies. Attached to it, as is often the case, is a workshop where "illusions" are manufactured. The craftsman who makes these and the proprietor of the shop are discussing a rather curious order which Esmeralda has just put in. She has supplied certain specifications, but has not explained what she wants to do, and the man who constructs apparatus is in some doubt as to how to proceed. It comes out in the course of the conversation that they do not quite like Esmeralda. At this moment, Esmeralda herself arrives to inspect what is being done. Baldini now also drops in. Esmeralda is not very cordial and does not talk about her project; but Baldini, who is mesmerized by her, is deferential toward her reticence, since it is customary for inventive magicians to keep their secrets at first from their colleagues. I do not know what Ed would have made of this, but my idea was to have it later suspected by Baldini when he is coming to rebel against Esmeralda's domination, that, in pretending to make him disappear in full sight of the audience, she

is preparing to do something dangerous. He is put on his
guard by the men in the shop, who are coming to have
some inkling of the nature of the contemplated "illusion."
What has happened is that Esmeralda has learned from
the head glassblower, whose hobby is physics, how to
vaporize in an instant on a limited scale. A flash and
some smoke will be seen by the audience, and Baldini
will have disappeared. Esmeralda, it turns out, is a fanat-
ical manhater, on account of having been sent, as an
orphan, to live with an uncle who raped her. The new
destructive powers she has now acquired are prompting
her to give vent to her lifelong antagonism by more and
more extravagant feats. Could she not make the glassblowers themselves disappear? They are to open up the
performance with a prelude for what is to come, by blowing up their glass bubbles till they burst with a bang.
Why not vaporize Derek, too? He along with Baldini are
to be permitted to put on individual acts and to have their
little applause before her own great feats of annihilation.
Why not—her madness accelerates—turn the wonder-gun
on men in the audience, too? She comes out in a sweat
as she thinks of it. She tries to control herself, assure herself that the disappearance of Baldini alone may be accepted as a magician's secret, and his subsequent nonap-
pearance be explained away as a retirement from the
profession on account of illness. She has yielded to Baldini's desire for the Solomon and Sheba spectacle. She,
as Sheba, will top Solomon's magic by making him vanish
in a puff. She grimly enjoys this prospect. But Baldini, by
the time of the performance, has been tipped off by the
magic-shop men that Esmeralda is mad as a hatter. He
has had her watched: a diary has been read, and her
lethal intentions have been discovered. Just before the
Solomon and Sheba act, her gun has been confiscated.
She is arrested and put under restraint barely in time to

avert the massacre. But the show must still go on. It is
announced that Esmeralda is ill, and one of the girl assistants acts as her understudy. Irena has had also to be
restrained and has bitten a policeman's wrist. The performance ends successfully with the spectacular finale,
which involves the girls doing cartwheels, the appearance
of cobras from baskets, and the production of national
banners, including both the Israel and the Arab flags, but
not those of the Communist countries or Franco's Spain.
Baldini, in the costume of Solomon, is the hero of this
dazzling number and takes the bows at the end, with a
speech in a heavy Yiddish accent. But Derek Marchmont
has climbed up on the elephant, which has been made to
reappear, and is waving the Union Jack.

At the time that Ed and I were discussing the revival
of Baldini, I received the following letter accompanied by
a glossy photograph of a very third-rate-looking dancer
majestically posed in a lace mantilla:

> January 24, 1967
> (NEW STYLE)

My dear, dear Mr. Wilson,

I am writing to you on this occasion because I have
only in the week just past received the most joyful news
that you are proposing to lend your magnificent talent to
a book about my son, otherwise perhaps known to you as
"Jack Baldini." Surely you will sense at once with your
keen eye that this is a genuine letter from an A-Number-
One mother, for the accompanying photograph, taken
only a *very few years ago,* is my darling son's favorite of
me, which he always kept very close to his person in his
boudoir.

I must tell you I took the occasion to write first to
your friendly collaborator, Mr. Edwin O'Connor, that

highly gifted man. He said I should immediately write
to you because of the purpose of my entreaty. He said to
me, he said, "Wilson is the money man, my dear lady; I
deal only in ideas!"

Accordingly then, to you I write. Naturally a book provided by you for the markets of the world, about such a
son of such a mother, can be expected to realize much in
the way of valuable moneys. Although I am of course an
*artiste* and under most circumstances cannot trouble my
pretty head with such bagatelles, just for fun, for a singing lark, as you Americans sometimes express it, I think
I would like to ask you for a small part of those moneys.
A novice in these crude affairs, I hardly know what next
to say; perhaps "fifty percent" would not be amiss?

My my, what a happy time we will have, all working
together! I intend to spend most days of the spring and
summer months very close to you on that blessed spit of
sand, Cape Cod. I will be in residence at the Hotel Holi-
day from Memory Day, May 30th; I will be accompanied
by a young Polish boy of nineteen whose spiritual counsel
I now feel indispensable. It is sad I will not have the
distinct pleasure of seeing Mr. O'Connor there, as he has
courteously explained to me that frequent family deaths
oblige him to journey to Japan for most of the coming
year.

Goodbye for now, dear Mr. Wilson! How I look forward to receiving a missive in your own hand, addressed
to me in care of my attorneys-at-law, Greenbaum, Wolff
& Ernst, in the city of New York, N.Y. Such pleasant
men they are, to be sure, but how harsh and unforgiving
if a crafty person should attempt to deprive a deserving
and quite beautiful woman of what is so rightfully hers.

> With all my cordiality,
> [Signature undecipherable]

This nonsense was not to be continued, and the break with all the other elements in one's friendly relations with Ed, the abrupt obliteration of his presence, his personality, was shocking to all who knew him. His death made a terrible vacancy in our little community at Wellfleet. As Mrs. Arthur Schlesinger, Jr., has written, in an article in the Boston *Globe*, he had become a kind of center of our life on the beach, where he knocked off to read in the afternoon after doing his work in the morning. One always had with him entertaining conversations, and his sustained imaginative activity was backed by an impressive physique. He three times saved bathers from being swept away. I once saw him swim out and pull in a raft with two girls which was being carried off to sea. I was struck by the fact that many people on the shore who had stood around watching this immediately disappeared when the raft had been safely brought in, without anyone's making any move to inquire about or offer anything to revive the two girls and Ed, who were lying on the sand exhausted. He scolded the girls for their recklessness, and the last time he rescued one of these greenhorns, he swore that he had "had it" as a lifeguard and would never rescue anyone again. He had undergone, before his marriage, a serious operation, the removal of a part of his stomach, but he seemed to have recovered so completely that one forgot that his condition might still be precarious. Since he has gone, I have been constantly reminded that Ed's death was a serious personal loss when I have from time to time caught myself still thinking, "I must tell Ed that," or, "I must ask Ed about this." I had by that time become interested in what was happening in the Catholic Church, and in talking to Ed about it, I found that he was capable of being just as sardonic about its ministrants as he was about anyone else. I believe that the explanation of his satirical children's fable *Benjy*—the story of a horrid little prig who makes trouble for everyone else—is that Ed was always on his guard about letting people be conscious of his virtuous habits because he realized how easy it would be for these to become obnoxious. He neither smoked nor drank; he was considerate and incorruptible. Though he never at all emphasized this and though he reacted very strongly to a badly performed Mass, he remained a practicing Catholic, and he was one of the few educated friends I have had who struck me as sincerely attempting to lead the life of a Christian. It was only when he died that one realized how much he had become in Boston a kind of public figure. His funeral was almost on the scale of that of a respected bishop or cardinal; and it was not merely his literary talents, his enlivening wit, his conspicuous commercial success, and his sympathetic capacity for fellowship with all classes and callings in the city that had made him such a popular personality but, together with all these attractive features, the reassuring sense that came through, from behind his satiric humor, of decency, reliability and an unwillingness to take ignoble advantage of the failings and misfortunes of other people. In spite of the egoistic old men, the virulent old women of his novels, he could hardly have allowed Esmeralda to have become such a monster as I was projecting, and I believe that it was partly this divergence of temperaments that brought our Baldini to a standstill.

# THE FRUITS OF THE MLA

## I

*The New York Review* of January 18, 1967, contained an article by Mr. Lewis Mumford called "Emerson Behind Barbed Wire," in which he reviewed *The Journals and Miscellaneous Notebooks of Ralph Waldo Emerson,* edited by five scholars and published by the Harvard University Press. Mr. Mumford attacked this edition on the ground that it included too much material which Emerson had left directions to destroy and that it had presented this material in a totally unreadable text, the editor of which, by resorting to no less than twenty diacritical marks, had made it look like something between an undecoded Morse message and a cuneiform inscription.

I applauded this article in a letter in which I criticized the prevailing practice of the Modern Language Association in reprinting the American classics and explained that I myself had had a project for publishing these classics in an easily accessible form, such as that of the French Pléiade series, and that I had at one time persuaded a number of people, publishers, writers, and foundation administrators—some of them members of the Council of the National Endowment of the Humanities —that such a collection would be very desirable in view

of the fact that the complete works of so many of the
American writers who are at present most talked about
and taught are unavailable to the ordinary reader. In order
to make my position clear, I am printing the letter that I
sent to Mr. Jason Epstein of Random House, which was
sent to the persons mentioned below.

August 18, 1962

Dear Jason:

I am glad to hear that you are going to take up with the
Bollingen Foundation the possibility of bringing out in a
complete and compact form the principal American
classics. I have, as you know, been trying for years to
interest some publisher in this project. It is absurd that
our most read and studied writers should not be available
in their entirety in any convenient form. For example,
the only collected edition of Melville was published in
England in the twenties and has long been out of print;
and there is not, and has never been, of Henry James
and Henry Adams any complete collected edition at all.
The only serious attempt, on any large scale, to do reliable editions of our classics was the publication by
Houghton Mifflin of such New England writers as
Emerson, Thoreau, and Hawthorne, and these are now
out of print. For years there was no scholarly edition of
Poe which even aimed at completeness and accuracy except that by James A. Harrison of the University of
Virginia, which has also been out of print—though I
understand that Mabbott of Columbia is about to bring
out a new one through the Harvard University Press.*
The collected Stephen Crane was published by Knopf
in a limited edition which can only be found in large
libraries.

The kind of thing I should like to see would follow the

* Professor Thomas O. Mabbott recently died, and the edition
has never been published (1968).

example of the Editions de la Pléiade, which have included so many of the French classics, ancient and modern, in beautifully produced and admirably printed thin-
paper volumes, ranging from 800 to 1500 pages. These
volumes, published by Gallimard, have evidently been
commercially successful, for they are to be seen in every
bookstore in Paris. Mondadori of Milan has been publishing two similar series of Classici Italiani and Classici
Contemporanei Italiani, though not on the same scale.
But Benedetto Croce persuaded another publisher, La-
terza, to bring out the series called *Scrittori d'Italia* as
well as a philosophical series, the former of which includes such not easily available works as Sarpi's histories
and the macaronic poets. In England, the Oxford University Press has brought out the English poets and a certain
amount of prose in cheap and well-edited volumes. Only
the United States, at a time when the interest in our literature has never been so keen, has nothing at all similar.
Parkman, for example, now much talked about, is, I believe, available only in paperback with the *Oregon Trail*
and a few volumes of his history. There has never been
a complete collected edition that included his novel and
his book on rose culture. In the case of many writers of
not necessarily the first importance, but such as are often
included in the Pléiade series, there exist—except for
random reprints by university presses, and occasionally
by paperback publishers—no modern editions at all. Such
writers need not be printed in toto, but there are several
which should have a volume of selections—John W.
De Forest, George Cable, Henry Fuller, Harold Frederic,
John Jay Chapman, Kate Chopin, and others. Certain
poets such as Emily Dickinson, Frederick Tuckerman,
and Trumbull Stickney should also be made available.
Such a series as the John Harvard Library or the paperback series now being brought out by Hafner is not

able to cover this field, and in the former case gives in a single volume too little at too high a price.

Almost everything should be edited anew, as in the case of the Pléiade editions. It would be possible, thus, in some cases, to establish, as has been done with Proust, the only sound and full text that exists.

Of course, there would be questions of copyright, as in the case of Emily Dickinson's newly published poems or Mark Twain's posthumous writings, but these are the kind of thing that, after first being published in expensive editions, are likely afterward to be sold to the paperbacks, and they might just as well be sold to a series of classics.

I am told that it would be necessary to apply for a government subsidy; but I do not see why this should not be done. If we can squander billions of dollars on space rockets, nuclear weapons, and subsidies to backward countries, why should not the United States government do something to make American literature available? The French government has now for decades contributed to the publication of French history and literature. I am informed by M. André Malraux, Ministre d'Etat Chargé des Affaires Culturelles, that the French government at the present time, through a Caisse Nationale des Lettres, is contributing to the publication of the complete works of Ernest Renan, Gérard de Nerval, and Paul Verlaine; the correspondence of Balzac and Villiers de l'Isle-Adam; critical editions of Charles Nodier and Mme de Staël; learned works such as *L'Histoire des Monuments Détruits de l'Art Français;* bilingual editions and translations of such foreign writers as Goethe and Kleist, etc. I was rather surprised to learn that a new edition of *Les Stances* by Jean Moréas had been subsidized. But this volume of his is a landmark of the Parnassian school of poetry, and is needed in their courses by students. In

1939, however, only 309 copies were sold in 1960, 52; and in 1961, 24. In view of this, the publisher, the Mercure de France, applied to the government for aid in bringing out a new edition. Further projects are new critical editions of the complete works of Pascal and the complete correspondence of Voltaire, Chateaubriand, and Flaubert. Recent writers who have been aided by subsidies from the government in order to carry on their work are Blaise Cendrars, Louis Guilloux, Pierre-Jean Jouve, François Ponge, Yves Bonnefoy, André du Bouchet, Henri Thomas, Wladimir Weidlé, Loys Masson.

Our record in this department is, so far as I know, nil —except, perhaps, for the job of poetry librarian in the Library of Congress, which is given every year to a different poet.

The people to whom this letter was sent were W. H. Auden, Marius Bewley, R. P. Blackmur, Van Wyck Brooks, Alfred Kazin, President Kennedy, Robert Lowell, Perry Miller, Norman Holmes Pearson, John Crowe Ransom, Allen Tate, Lionel Trilling, Mark Van Doren, and Robert Penn Warren. Of these, only the late Perry Miller, a professor of American literature at Harvard, even mentioned the question of the difficulties of preparing authoritative texts—though he admitted that "the project on Hawthorne, to cite only this one, being undertaken by the University of Ohio is perhaps more 'academic' than the average reader needs." The others expressed cordial approval. The Bollingen Foundation decided that a project such as this did not come within the scope assigned to it; but I was told later that a substantial sum of money had been set aside for this purpose by the National Humanities Endowment, which was established as a part of the functioning of the National Foundation of the Arts and Humanities, the bill for which had been enacted by Congress in 1965. The next thing I heard about it was that this money had somehow been whisked away, and my project "tabled"—that is, set aside, dismissed. The Modern Language Association had, it seemed, had a project of its own for reprinting the American classics and had apparently had ours suppressed. The MLA, founded at Johns Hopkins in 1883, is in its way a formidable organization, to which, evidently, almost every teacher of literature or language is obliged to belong. It publishes a periodical usually known as *PMLA* (*Publications of the Modern Language Association*), which contains for the most part unreadable articles on literary problems and discoveries of very minute or no interest. An annual countrywide conference of the MLA is held during the Christmas holidays and is attended by from five to ten thousand people, and there are also regional conferences. At all of these, papers are read, which have been or are to be published in *PMLA* or some other learned periodical. In the program of the First Annual Conference of 1968 of the New York–Pennsylvania branch, forty-nine such papers were featured. The list is too long to quote here. A few of them I should look at if I saw them, because I happen to have lately given attention to their subjects: "Madach's *Tragedy of Man* and German Literature" and "Comparison of Goethe's Mephistopheles and Balzac's Vautrin"; others I think I should skip: "Flowers, Women, and Song in the Poetry of William Carlos Williams," and "The Unity of George Peele's *The Old Wives Tale*." But my point of view about these papers is almost entirely irrelevant because they are meant not to appeal to any possible interest in them on the part of such people as me, but to serve as offered self-qualifications in what is really an employment agency. The head of a department attends the conference in order to fill some chair when an occupant has been discarded or has been lured away by higher pay to some other institution; the candidate is attempting to impress the employer by displaying some of his wares. This is all, of course, perfectly legitimate; the Modern Language Association has no doubt performed a useful role. But what I want to deal with here is the ineptitude of its pretensions to reprint the American classics.

To return to Mr. Mumford's article and my letter giving voice to my own complaints, these provoked a remarkable correspondence, some of which has been printed in *The New York Review*. First of all, Mr. William M. Gibson, whose name heads the list of scholars that are responsible for the editing of the Emerson papers and who is, it turns out, the Director of the MLA Center for the Editions of American Authors, wrote me that he had no idea what had happened to the money we were supposed to get. I knew, however, that the MLA had a strong and determined lobby to further its own designs and that representatives of the MLA had attempted to discourage our project and had, it seems, very soon succeeded. Mr. Gibson also wrote a long letter to the editors of *The New York Review,* which was published in the issue of March 14, 1968. He argued here with a rhetoric almost Ciceronian that "there is no serious difference between Mr. Mumford's view and the views" of the MLA editors: "Mr. Mumford wants accurate unexpurgated texts: so do the editors. Mr. Mumford especially wants the text uncluttered with revisions or footnote numbers or any kind of 'barbed wire'; so do the editors." He says that the Center editors want to produce the "clear text" that "Mr. Mumford favors"—"clear text," sometimes hyphenated, is a part of this scholarly jargon and seems to mean simply a readable book; *but* the task of their peculiar kind of editing must be accomplished *"first"* (Mr. Gibson's italics) before a "clear text" can be

made that will "serve the interest of scholars and plain
readers alike." But in the meantime, we shall have to
wait a century or longer before, according to the requirements imposed by the MLA, such texts will become available, and in the case of each $10 volume, two years, it is
stipulated, will have to elapse before a commercial publisher will be allowed to take them over. So Mr. Mumford and the MLA do *not* want the same thing.

Mr. M. H. Abrams and Mr. Morton W. Bloomfield,
of Cornell and Harvard respectively, are more briefly and
bluntly self-defensive. They are "surprised" at Lewis
Mumford and me. Are they really to understand that we
"believe it is better to make available to the public texts
which these authors did not write, or which they wrote
only in part?" This sounds as if there were discrepancies
as great between the extant texts and those the MLA is
preparing as between, say, Laforgue's softened and polished version of Casanova's memoirs and the original
Brockhaus text that has only lately come to light, or that
it had just been discovered that *The Gilded Age* was
written by Mark Twain in collaboration with Charles
Dudley Warner—which is a ridiculous exaggeration.
Can these scholars of Cornell and Harvard provide us
with actual examples of such serious suppressions and
distortions?

Other letters from MLA editors seem to betray an uneasy sense of guilt. A long epistle from a "Center for
Textual Studies" by a man whom I have never met and
of whom I have never heard begins with what I suppose
to be meant as a propitiatory paragraph, in which he pro-
fesses to envy me my enjoyment of spring on Cape Cod—
which is actually rather bleak—since the part of the
Middle West to which he is at present condemned cannot
be said to have a spring. The roses, he says, do not bloom
out there nor have the lilies any fragrance. Yet his fa-

vorite locality, he says, is not Cape Cod but Plum Island off Newburyport. A description of this follows. But in paragraph three he gets down to business. He proceeds to confuse the issue. He believes that he and I are really, as Mr. Gibson believes that he and Mr. Mumford are, in fundamental agreement. He is one of a team of thirty-five scholars who are working on the Mark Twain papers. He acknowledges that this project is "a boondoggle" —the verb is defined in Macmillan's Modern Dictionary as "to do (and be paid public money for) trivial or unnecessary work." It seems that eighteen of these Mark Twain workers are reading *Tom Sawyer,* word by word, backward, in order to ascertain, without being diverted from this drudgery by attention to the story or the style, how many times "Aunt Polly" is printed as "aunt Polly," and how many times "ssst!" is printed as "sssst!" It seems that "a careful check on a Hinman Collating Machine" has shown that, in the text of *Tom Sawyer,* there are not really any serious problems about either the state or the text or the alterations Mark Twain made in it. This boondoggling, the writer of the letter explains, is a natural consequence of a new federal program called "work-study," by which the government puts up eighty-five percent of what the students earn by academic work. But who decides the kind of work they do? The MLA acting through the government? The writer does not make this plain. He disapproves of what is being done and has ideas for improving the situation. I hope that I am not violating his confidence in making public the substance of what he has written me; but I take it that his letter is in the nature of an open plaint, and I assume that he would not have been at pains to describe the situation so carefully if he had not been willing to have me make use of the information.

The writers of other letters have enthusiastically seconded my recommendation that an overall library of the American classics should immediately be begun and be put as soon as possible on the market. A typical example of these supporters is a teacher of American Literature from Queens College, New York, who is at present a Fulbright lecturer in Tokyo. She writes me that it is bad enough, when teaching at home, to have difficulty in getting for one's students the works of Poe, Melville, Hawthorne, and James, but that it is even more vexatious and embarrassing not to be able to provide her students in Japan with anything but a few scrappy reprints of the great American writers whom she is supposed to be leading them to appreciate. "Both members of my family and close friends have benefited from the academic editing industry, so I really do know how accurate you are in that letter."

The latest products of the MLA editions have been Herman Melville's *Typee,* edited by three professors, with a fourth as "Bibliographical Associate" and a fifth as "Contributor of the Historical Note," published by Northwestern University Press in association with the Newberry Library; the fourth volume of the Centenary Edition of the Works of Nathaniel Hawthorne, published with the sanction of half-a-dozen editors, by the Ohio State University Press; and William Dean Howells's *Their Wedding Journey,* edited by John K. Reeves, with the support of a "Textual Editor" and two assistant "Textual Editors." Each of these volumes is stamped with a kind of official imprimatur: AN APPROVED TEXT. MODERN LANGUAGE ASSOCIATION OF AMERICA. I propose to disapprove, and I shall begin with *Their Wedding Journey,* which is certainly the *reductio ad absurdum* of the practice of the MLA. It is announced as the first volume of a forty-volume selection from Howells, but the number on the spine is "5." Now, *Their Wedding Jour-*

*ney* was Howells's first published novel, and it is hard to imagine which volumes of his earlier published work could be made to run to four volumes. This is, in any case, the first step in an operation under the general editorship of Edwin H. Cady, Rudy Professor of English at Indiana University, assisted by an editorial board. This series is to be published by the Indiana University Press. I learn from a publicity handout that this publication of the first of these volumes was nothing less than "a momentous occasion for the entire staff. To celebrate, Professor Cady was host at a party attended by I.U. [Indiana University] President Elvis J. Stahr and other officials. And just to be sure the editors were still on their toes, Mrs. Cady brought forth a festive cake on which was described in pink frosting, 'The Weeding (cq) Journey.' The error was caught in far less than five successive readings." I suppose I understand the joke, but what does "(cq)" mean? * It does seem perhaps unfortunate that so many of these MLA volumes should be products of the Middle West.

In the first place, what is the point of reprinting this first novel of Howells at all? It is one of his least interesting books. What, especially, is the point of reprinting it with thirty-five pages of textual commentary which record the variations of nine of the existing texts? We are told in the bulletin quoted above that "Howells spelled 'millionaire' with two *n*'s, and sometimes used a comma-dash"—as did many of the writers of his period. What is the desirability of retaining Howells's spelling of "millionaire" or even his comma-dashes? Mr. Reeves announces in his introduction that "in view of Howells's eventual distinction as a realistic novelist, it is particularly fortunate that materials have survived which enable us

* I have learned that it is a newspaper notation meaning "correct"—that is, "Follow copy."

to trace the process by which he transformed his travel experience into his first successful piece of fiction. These materials are: (1) travel articles which as a young correspondent Howells had written for the *Ohio State Journal* and the Cincinnati *Gazette* in the summer of 1860, when on his famous pilgrimage to New England he covered some of the same ground over which he later sent his honeymooners; (2) a diary of 'last summer's travels' (i.e. 1870), which took him and Mrs. Howells over the entire route of the wedding journey; (3) a brief diary of a trip to Niagara Falls with his father probably in the early summer of 1871; and (4) the working manuscript of the novel." We learn that Mr. William M. Gibson, of whom I have already spoken as director of and apologist for the MLA, has already made "a detailed study of Howells's use of the travel articles in the early novels. He estimates that about a tenth of *Their Wedding Journey* was drawn, often verbatim, from these newspaper pieces. Later, when the manuscript came to light, printed portions of these articles were in fact pasted into the text."

What on earth is the interest of all this? Every writer knows how diaries and articles are utilized as material for books, and no ordinary reader knows or cares. What is important is the finished work by which the author wishes to stand. All this scholarship squandered on *Their Wedding Journey* is a waste of money and time. We are told that all nineteen of the people in the Worcester Depot in Boston who appear in the *Wedding Journey* had been noted in Howells's diary, but that "several figures in the diary do not appear in the novel." Three pages are devoted to "Word-Division." These attempt to show the proper policy for dealing with compound words when they are broken at the end of a line. The editor has to find out how they are printed, with or without a hyphen, when they are not broken up in this way. The "Notes to the Text" are meager: they explain quotations and allusions and matters of punctuation and spelling. But in connection with a description of what Howells calls a "conventional American hotel clerk," who is said to exhale "from his person . . . the mystical odors of Ihlang-ihlang," Mr. Reeves, in his notes on hyphens, rather unnecessarily establishes that "Ihlang-ihlang" is to be hyphenated even when it is not split in two at the end of a line, without any attempt to tell us what Ihlang-ihlang is—a perfume or a face lotion? a real product or an invention of Howells's? and if an invention, a parody of what? *

In Mr. Reeves's introduction, there is very little of literary interest. He explains that *Their Wedding Journey* marks the point at which the Howells who wrote the travel sketches modulated into the writer of novels, and he gives some examples of the favorable comments that the book received when it was published in 1871. It was republished several times and became very popular as a wedding present. I read it in an edition of 1894, obviously intended for this purpose, with gilt edges and a white and gilt cover and with up-to-date illustrations in which the characters wear the costumes of the nineties instead of the original illustrations in which the ladies wore the hoopskirts of the seventies, which are mentioned at one point in the text. I noted that, in Chapter 4, the word "amazement" had been printed for "amusement," and I looked at once at the new edition to see whether the textual editor had caught this error. He had. But Mr. Reeves, in his introduction, totally ignores the fact that *Their Wedding Journey* was followed in 1900 by a sequel, *Their Silver Wedding Journey,* in which the same

* A correspondent informs me that Ihlang-ihlang is "an aromatic oil used in perfume."

couple, Basil and Isabel March, travel to Austria and Germany instead of to Canada and Niagara Falls. I should think that if there were any reason for reprinting the first *Journey* at all, it ought to be combined with the second, since together they illustrate the aging of what can be called a happy marriage. The second of them is actually more interesting than the first, because the story is more complex and presents a greater variety of American types. Nor is the special importance of the Marches to Howells's whole work explained. Mr. Reeves does note that the Marches "were found so useful [by Howells] for creating fiction out of his actual experience that he used them in eight more stories at various times in his career." But why does he not tell us which these stories are? And why does he not emphasize that Basil March is to become the central figure, when the Marches are made to immigrate, like the Howellses, to New York from Boston, in one of Howells's most read novels, *A Hazard of New Fortunes?*

I have read both these wedding journeys with a mild, rather cozy interest of tranquillity recollected in tranquillity. I myself, at a not much later period—at least one in which things had not yet much changed—have waited in upstate New York railroad stations, made a steamboat trip down the St. Lawrence, on which I bought beadwork from an Indian woman, and visited Montreal and Quebec; I, too, have spent part of a summer in Carlsbad and stayed at Pupp's Hotel and had breakfast out of doors at the Freundschaftsaal, "done" Nuremberg, Cologne, and Frankfurt, and made a sightseeing trip down the Rhine— so I could check my own childhood memories of the early 1900's with the contemporary impressions of mature minds. These "journeys" are also documents on the American consciousness of its relation to Europe. In the first of them, the Marches, who had already been abroad, are constantly looking in America for approximations to what they regard as the superior picturesqueness of Europe. Of the chapel at Laval University in Quebec: "There was nothing in the place that need remind them of America, and its taste was exactly that of a thousand other churches of the eighteenth century." They greatly admired in Quebec the "thick-ankled" French Canadian "peasants"; but, on their way back to Buffalo (on a subsequent journey twelve years later), they "owned that this railroad suburb had its own impressiveness, and they said that the trestle-work was as noble in effect as the lines of aqueduct that stalk across the Roman Campagna." But in the later book, the Marches are comparing American and European habits and institutions in a more nearly objective and critical way. They do not approve of the German carts that are drawn by a dog and a woman, the lack of heating in German hotels or the hideous militaristic monuments; but they like the once princely parks and gardens now converted into "the playground of the landless poor" and reflect that they "did not know why Goethe should be held personally responsible for the existence of the woman-and-dog team." Aside from such considerations, I cannot imagine why anyone except devoted specialists in Howells should take the trouble to read these tepid books—especially at the price of ten dollars apiece as the cost of hyphen-hunting and regularizing the spelling.

The MLA volume of Melville's *Typee* has three professors listed as editors, together with a "Bibliographical Associate" and a "Contributor of the Historical Note." The Historical Note is meager, and it is followed by seventy-one pages of MLA textual notes. There does exist a slight textual problem here that has to be dealt with seriously. The original manuscript, except for one page, has disappeared. The book was first published in

England, and the later American edition was somewhat purged in the interests of propriety. Melville afterward published in New York a new revised edition, omitting, as he explains, certain passages, with an appendix irrelevant to the narrative proper and with a few alterations in style. In 1922, the English publisher Constable began bringing out the now out-of-print but still only complete collected Melville. In this set, the text is different from any other: it follows in general practice the original English text, but in parts the American revised one, and shows some new emendations of its own.

All this did certainly need straightening out, but the editors make very heavy weather of it. What to do about the inconsistency in the first American edition in spelling nouns that end in *-or* or *-our* or verbs that end in *-ize* or *-ise*? And then there is the great hyphenization problem: "The missing hyphen in *married* at E213-2 [191.34] is also obvious, since the word is not a compound." I am prepared to acknowledge the competence of Mr. Harrison Hayford, Mr. Hershel Parker, and Mr. G. Thomas Tasello in the deadening task assigned to them (though they do not seem to have noted that Melville's reference to Chapter 3 in the fifth line from the bottom of page 312 ought to have been to Chapter 4). I am told that these MLA editors are the constant recipients of edicts in which the management lays down to them the principles on which they must proceed in their work, and that they are sometimes as much bored and annoyed by them as one would imagine them to be; but the project in the case of *Typee* has been so relentlessly carried out in the technical language of this species of scholarship—of "substantives," "accidentals," and "copy-texts"—that a glossary should be provided for readers who are not registered union members—if there are any such readers—of the Modern Language Association. The great demiurge be-

hind all this editing seems to be Mr. Fredson Bowers of
the University of Virginia. I am on friendly terms with
Mr. Bowers, and I know that he is an impassioned bibli-
ographer as well as an expert on Elizabethan texts, a field
where it seems to me his attentions would have a better
chance of proving valuable than in the checking of
American ones. I have been told that his lectures on bibliography are so thrilling that young students often leave
them with no other ambition than to become master bibliographers. But I have found no reason to believe that
he is otherwise much interested in literature. It has been
said, in fact, I believe, by someone in the academic world
that, in editing *Leaves of Grass,* he had done everything
for it but read it.

The Historical Note for *Typee* by Mr. Leon Howard
of the University of California is informative as far as it
goes. He deals briefly with the interesting question of
how much of *Typee* is based on actual experience, how
much derived from other books, and how much supplied
by imagination. It is, one supposes, impossible completely
to disentangle these elements, yet one would have liked
to have some checking and commentary by an anthropologist who knows Polynesia. One could not, I suppose,
however, expect that the MLA would care to humiliate
its Hinman Collating Machine by associating it with a
raw anthropologist.

Both these volumes have the common American fault
—*Typee* even more than *Their Wedding Journey*—of
being too large and heavy to hold and being set with too
wide a page for the eye to travel from one line to the
next without effort. But the fourth volume of the Centenary Edition of the works of Nathaniel Hawthorne,
which contains only *The Marble Faun,* is the masterpiece
of MLA bad bookmaking. I have weighed it, and it
weighs nine pounds. It is 9 by 6⅛ inches, and 2⅜

inches thick. The paper is heavy and grayish. I first read *The Marble Faun* on a plane coming back from Italy, in an English pocket edition from Bohn's Popular Library, "reprinted from the first published, with such slight alterations from the American edition as appear to have resulted from the author's own revision"—having read the "New England Romances" also in a pocket edition, also published in England, but imported over here by Scribners. This volume belonged to a more elegant series whose format more or less represents the kind of thing I have had in mind for a series of the American classics. It was printed on thin paper and bound in blue leather—size 7¼ inches by 3¾, weight hardly one pound. Its 713 pages contained all three of these novels. If one made the books a little fatter, one certainly could get the whole of Hawthorne into two Pléiade-size volumes. (A "Preface to the Text" in the new edition states that it will provide "established texts of the romances, tales, and associated shorter works." What does "associated" mean? Are we not to have the whole of Hawthorne?) But the Centenary edition of *The Marble Faun,* since it is mainly Mr. Bowers's work, embodies the spirit of Mr. Bowers as no other of these volumes does. Of its 610 pages, the 467 of Hawthorne are weighed down by 89 pages of "Textual Introduction" and 143 pages of "Textual Notes." There are 44 pages of historical introduction preceding the textual introduction. We are told in these introductions, in accordance with the MLA formula, that, in the course of writing the book, the author, as novelists often do, changed the names of certain of the characters; and that many of the descriptions in it—as has been noted, also a common practice—have been taken from his Italian notebooks. This information is of no interest whatever. Nor is it of any interest to be told that Hawthorne's wife corrected certain inaccuracies in

the Roman descriptions and otherwise made occasional
suggestions, which Hawthorne did not always accept. It
has evidently been trying for Mr. Bowers to find that, in
the original manuscript, the author had been so incon-
siderate as usually to make his changes "by wiping out
with a finger while the ink was still wet and writing over
the same space." But the places where these smudges
occur have been carefully noted and listed. (It seems to
me that this whole procedure meets an unsurmountable
obstacle when no corrected proofs survive that show the
revisions of the author.)

Now, what conceivable value have 276 pages of all
this? Surely only that of gratifying the very small group
of monomaniac bibliographers. I do not, of course, deny
that the scrutinizing of variants may, in some cases, be of
interest. Where a mystery is involved, as in *Edwin Drood*
or *The Turn of the Screw,* the revisions by the author
of his manuscript or first edition may throw light upon
his intention. In other cases, the revelation of the methods shown by successive rewritings may have something to teach other writers. *Dernières Pages Inédites
d'Anatole France,* intelligently edited by Michel Corday,
prints, from an unfinished dialogue, several versions of
an ironic passage on Kant that shows him, after the long
cogitations that produced his philosophic system, falling
back on a conventional view of God. Here a longer and
fuller statement is gradually reduced to forty-nine words.
And in the volume of the manuscripts of *Madame Bovary* published by Jean Pommier and Gabrielle Leleu,
we see that the most beautiful passages that have stuck
in one's mind like poetry—Charles Bovary in his boyhood looking wistfully out the window, the old farm
servant at the Comices getting an award for her years of
service—one finds that it was Flaubert's practice to begin with an accumulation of accurate realistic details,

and that the poetry came much later and involved elim-
ination of many of these details. The definitive text of
Proust in the Pléiade, which I believe cost its two editors
ten years of work, is the only text that should be read.
The last volumes of À la Recherche were published after
Proust's death and much edited by Gallimard for easy
consumption. Here you have these as Proust had to leave
them, as well as an omitted episode apparently withheld
from the earlier volumes, though reference is made to it
there, in order to introduce it later on when it would have
a more shocking effect. The variants, too, have a curious
interest. If the printer garbled something or left something
out, Proust did not refer to his manuscript to find out what
he had written but filled in with something else. And
then there is the case of the Russian writers, such as Pushkin and Tolstoy, who were censored by the Czar's censor.
The Soviets, in excellent editions, have now published
these cut or altered passages—though they have made
some suppressions of their own in the case of Chekhov's
letters.

Mr. Mumford made a very important point in the
second of his letters to *The New York Review* in the
course of the controversy aroused by his article. He said
that we do not want served up to us the writer's rejected
garbage. He had no doubt shuddered at the thought—
which is likely to trouble any careful writer—that all his
early notes and drafts might survive and fall into the
hands of the MLA editors or be handed over to those of
young Ph.D. candidates, who could only benefit from
them—the brighter ones—by becoming convinced of the
absurdity of our oppressive Ph.D. system of which we
would have been well rid if, at the time of the First
World War, when we were renaming our hamburgers
Salisbury Steak and our sauerkraut Liberty Cabbage, we
had decided to scrap it as a German atrocity. The indis-

criminate greed for this literary garbage on the part of
the universities is a sign of the academic pedantry on
which American Lit. has been stranded. It requires discrimination to understand the difference in value between, on the one hand, the drafts of an unfinished work
by Anatole France exhibited as *exercices de style* and the
manuscripts of *Madame Bovary,* so long and so exactingly
labored on, and, on the other hand, the relation of *Their
Wedding Journey* to Howells's travel notes and the variants of its reprintings. But of anything like discrimination
these MLA editors do not have a gleam, or if they have,
they are afraid to reveal it.

## II

I have already discussed the advisability of printing an
author's notes and early drafts—that is, what Lewis Mumford calls his "garbage." This question is raised by Mr.
Franklin R. Rogers at the beginning of his introduction to
Mark Twain's *Satires and Burlesques,* one of the volumes
of Mark Twain's hitherto unpublished papers which are
being brought out in fourteen volumes, under the aus-
pices of the Modern Language Association, by the University of California Press. "It should always be with
some misgivings," Mr. Rogers confesses, "that an editor
presents to the public materials which the author has discarded. By returning the materials to his files, the author
has voted against publication. By resurrecting them, the
editor risks exposing the author to the adverse criticism
which he wished to avoid. But at the same time, the resurrection serves a valuable purpose by making available
almost indispensable evidence to be used by those seek-
ing to understand the creative process." In this case, Mr.
Rogers claims that the many false starts and imperfect
pieces that have been collected here show that it was
not true that Mark Twain, as he sometimes pretended,
found it easy to tell a story, that, on the contrary, he

often found great difficulty in getting one under way. A parody of Victor Hugo, he believes, throws some light on Mark Twain's attitude toward the South in the Civil War and toward the policies of the Republicans afterward. But beyond this, for the ordinary reader, who is not obliged to use them for a Ph.D. thesis, these papers have no interest whatever. If he has already looked into this author's complete works, he knows that Mark Twain, during his lifetime, had already published so much now uninteresting clowning that there can be very little point in salvaging any he rejected.

In the volume of Mark Twain's *Letters to His Publishers,* edited by Mr. Hamlin Hill and published in the same series, there is ample evidence that, as Mr. Hill begins by saying in his introduction, "It was a dangerously dehumanizing experience to be Mark Twain's publisher," since you were likely to be subjected to abuse that suggests the zoological denunciations which are standard in the Soviet Union. One of his publishers is "not a man, but a hog"; his successor is called a tadpole. Of the first of these he writes to his brother, "I have never hated any creature with a hundred thousand fraction of the hatred which I bear that human louse Webster"; and of another man he writes that he "was a tall, lean, skinny, yellow, toothless, bald-headed, rat-eyed professional liar and scoundrel . . . I have had contact with several conspicuously mean men, but they were noble compared to this bastard monkey." Mr. Hill believes, no doubt correctly, that Mark Twain's fury against these publishers was at least partly due to their failure to make as much money out of his books as he had hoped, and that this fury was especially embittered by a resentment within himself "toward the commercial aspect of his own personality." He sometimes blames them for losing money through courses he had himself suggested.

All this matter would be useful to a biographer, and it

is perhaps just as well to have it on record. But some of Mark Twain's unpublished papers have another and more serious kind of importance. They contain a good deal of material that is of special interest to his admirers, because it is an integral part of his work, of his report on his own life, which his own inhibitions at first against making known his real unconventional ideas about sex and religion in America and his feelings about accepted public figures prevented him from publishing during his lifetime. Later on, after his death, their publication was long held up by similar inhibitions on the part of his surviving daughter. His philosophic dialogues called *What Is Man?*, which expounded a blind determinism, he had printed in a private edition, which he distributed among his friends. It was published for general distribution only after his death in 1910, when its ideas were shocking to nobody, but revealed the gloomy conclusions to which he had at last been forced. In the same volume were included his darkest pages, his reflections on the death of his daughter Jean, which were to end the *Autobiography*. We must hope that this long autobiographical manuscript, which Mark Twain had begun in the seventies and to which he added much in his later years, is to be given to us at last as he left it. Mark Twain took it very seriously. He prefixed to it a "Preface as from the Grave," in which he says that from the grave he can at last "speak freely." "When a man is writing a book dealing with the privacies of his life—a book which is to be read while he is still alive—he shrinks from speaking his whole frank mind; all his attempts to do it fail, he recognizes that he is trying to do a thing which is wholly impossible to a human being."

Now, we have never had the whole of this work, but only three sets of selections from it: one edited by his first biographer, Albert Bigelow Paine, *Mark Twain's*

*Autobiography,* which is much censored and quite in-
nocuous; another, *Mark Twain in Eruption,* edited by
Bernard De Voto, which collects some rather derisive and
sometimes embittered descriptions of public figures whom
Mark Twain had known, such as Roosevelt, Carnegie,
and Bret Harte; and a third, *The Autobiography of
Mark Twain,* edited by Charles Neider and, contrary to
Mark Twain's wish, arranged in chronological order of
events instead of in the scrambled order in which he had
dictated the sections. Mr. Neider has included in his volumes some particularly injurious passages on such special *bête noires* of Mark Twain's as Bret Harte and Mrs.
Thomas Bailey Aldrich, but he leaves out a good many
other things. It is surely one of the prime duties of these
editors of the Mark Twain papers to give us a complete
and straight version, newspaper clippings and all, of the
whole of the autobiographical manuscript. One hopes that
this is what is promised by the University of California
Press when it announces three volumes of autobiography.

Another important section of Mark Twain's unpublished writings which has needed to be put in order and
made available is the nexus of manuscripts left as records
of his repeated attempts to write a difficult and disturbing novel which should give voice to the mood of despair
that produced *What Is Man?* and *The Death of Jean.*
The publication of these has also up to now been im-
peded by the objections of the Mark Twain Estate—objections presumably based on their uniform unpleasantness and skepticism. These fragments seem all to have
been written between 1896 and 1905. They have now
been collected by Mr. John S. Tuckey in a volume called
*Which Was the Dream? and Other Symbolic Writings
of the Later Years.* Mr. Tuckey has succeeded very ably
in disentangling this complicated cluster, in tracing the
relationships between the fragmentary narratives and

their relation to the tragic aspects of this period of Mark Twain's life. They are certainly of very great interest, and they ought, with the *Autobiography*, to be included —if we are ever to get one—in any Collected Works of Mark Twain.* (I think, however, that another piece now published for the first time complete in Mr. Tuckey's volume, *Three Thousand Years Among the Microbes*, might well be omitted from the canon. This satire on which Mark Twain, after his wife's death, worked one summer with such satisfaction and from which an excerpt had been printed at the end of Paine's biography, has been awaited with much curiosity, but it turns out to be disappointing. It is rambling and labored and boring. It displays at its very worst its author's incapacity for self-criticism.)

The best discussion I have seen—in fact, the only adequate discussion—of this confused and agonized phase of Mark Twain's life and writing is Bernard De Voto's chapter "The Symbols of Despair" in his volume called *Mark Twain at Work*. Mark Twain, after the early successes that made him rich and a public figure, lost his money by investing in a publishing business and an impracticable typesetting machine, and was subjected to heavy pressure under the obligation to pay his debts by lecturing that went against the grain and a kind of popular travel writing that bored him. He had established a beloved family in Hartford, Connecticut—where he had

* The University of California, apart from the MLA edition of the papers, has announced another series of Mark Twain's already published works. This is supposed to contain five volumes of Mark Twain's Collected Correspondence, the first two to appear in 1971, and the rest in 1972. But in the meantime various volumes of special groups of correspondence have appeared or are to appear in the "papers" series. Why not simply get to work on the comprehensive correspondence? Perhaps because getting it out thus piecemeal will provide more work for editors?

built for them a delightfully luxurious and highly individual house: it imitated the shape of a steamboat; but in 1896, when the Clemenses were on their travels, one of their daughters, left at home, died suddenly of meningitis; another had turned out to be an epileptic and died, in 1909, the day before Christmas, in one of her seizures. Olivia, Mark Twain's wife, broke down in 1902 from what were then called "heart disease" and "nervous prostration," and died after twenty-two months, during which her husband had sometimes for long intervals not been allowed to see her, except for a very few minutes on some such occasion as a wedding anniversary. He had shaken her religious faith and deprived her of belief in an afterlife, and he bitterly reproached himself for this. He had also reproached himself for his having been away at the time of Susy's death and for the death of their first child, a twenty-two-month-old son whom he had taken out on a winter day and allowed to become uncovered. His failures in his business ventures had brought hardships upon the family as well as humiliations to himself.

These years were thus tormented by a persistent sense of guilt, and all these writings are an attempt to project this. What is common to nearly all of them is the idea of a man involved in a dream—a kind of dream that gives the impression of lasting for many years but that has taken only a few minutes—in which his fine house is burned down and he and his family are reduced to poverty, or in which, though respected by everyone else, he is driven by the desire to keep up appearances into courses that are actually criminal. Mr. Tuckey, in his introduction, tells us that a visit to the Hartford house had evidently set off this fantasy. Mrs. Clemens, after Susy's death, could not bear to go on living there, so they had rented the house to friends. "It seemed," he wrote to Olivia, "as if I had burst awake out of a hellish dream, and had never been away, and that you had come drifting down out of those upper regions with the little children tagging after you." I think that De Voto was correct in believing that Mark Twain, who blamed himself for everything unfortunate that had happened to him, was continually trying to reconcile the prosperity and happiness of his earlier period with the anguish and loss of what followed. He had always made fun of "the Moral Sense," but his conviction of sin never left him. I agree with Bernard De Voto that the determinism of *What Is Man?* is an attempt to escape the necessity of this self-conviction of guilt by assuming that neither he nor anyone else is responsible for his actions, and that in his stories of the horrible dream in which the central character is made to realize that he could not have acted otherwise, Mark Twain is making an effort to alleviate his painful situation by suggesting that these miseries may be all a dream from which he will in time awake.

The titles of two of these unfinished stories, *Which Was the Dream?* and *Which Was It?* were meant to leave the reader in doubt. But what De Voto does not suggest —though it seems to me very plain—is that the pressure still operating in Mark Twain's mind, combated but never expelled, was the menacing theology of Calvinism. According to Calvin, you go to Hell unless previously, before you were born, you have been "elected" by God, and these unfortunate heroes of Mark Twain's aborted novels cannot be certain that they have been. When disasters had befallen Mark Twain, he had regarded them all as punishments for crimes of which he himself was guilty, because what he describes in his memoirs as his "trained Presbyterian conscience" had caused him to feel damned for original sin. It is insisted in *Which Was It?* again and again that the supposedly good man who pays a debt with counterfeit money and in consequence commits an unpremeditated murder is only acting like any other man who should be driven by the same temptations. It is significant that Mark Twain should include a drawing supposed to have been made by his sinner, in the tradition of the old allegorical prints representing sin as a tree, in which all of his sequence of misdemeanors is shown to have grown from their roots in "False Pride." In *The Mysterious Stranger,* says De Voto, Mark Twain does succeed in resolving his problem by imagining that the whole of life is a dream in the mind of an omnipotent Satan. This got rid of the conflict with God. It should be added that the "angry God" of Jonathan Edwards, who holds the non-elected sinners above the fiery pit, where the Devil "stands ready to fall upon them, and seize them as his own, at what moment God shall permit him," may easily be confused with him who had formerly been known as God's "Adversary."

This theme of the guilty dream took two forms in Mark Twain's mind. In one of these, that mentioned above, it is a question of a once prosperous or honorable family undone by a disastrous fire or an unconfessed murder. The various versions of this have many points of interest. Very soon after the beginning of one of them, which he very soon dropped, Mark Twain, in giving an account of the principal inhabitants of Indiantown, which is obviously derived from Hannibal, Missouri, the small town of Mark Twain's boyhood, seems to be thrown off the track in describing the relations of one David Gridley with his wife, a description which establishes quite definitely that Mark Twain, after his marriage, however much he loved Olivia and depended upon her for guidance, felt himself to have been involved in something of a double life. The "sham David" was his wife's invention, he was what she wanted him to be: a churchgoer who dressed "like a gentleman," who "traded in fine and delicate things only, and delivered them from his tongue aromatic with chaste fragrance." But "the real David had a native affection for all vulgarities, and his natural speech was at home and happy only when it was mephitic with them"; he was "a Vesuvius boiling to the brim with imprisoned profanity."

The longest of the developments of this theme, *Which Was It?*, which runs here to 250 pages, displays Mark Twain's familiar weaknesses: his inability to decide on a story line, which leads him into aimless digression, as well as his humorist's tendency to give way to burlesque exaggeration where credible characterization is needed. The story at first appears fairly plausible, but it then becomes very much less so—though of course we can never be sure that the events are supposed to have taken place: they may really be a complicated nightmare. There is one remarkable episode which, as Mr. Kenneth Lynn has pointed out,* is comparable only to the interchange of black and white roles in Melville's "Benito Cereno." A mulatto, repudiated by his white father, who has branded his mother as a slave, has found out the truth about the murder committed by the damned central character, whose illegitimate brother he is, and blackmails him into changing places with him, so that in public the master is to be master and the mulatto his humble servitor, while in private the mulatto is to be the master and to be given free rein to humiliate and bully his white half-brother. This episode is, I believe, the bitterest of Mark Twain's dramatizations of the relations of the whites with the blacks. Here the guilt that he seems always to have felt about this relation is made to feed the general sense of guilt that is tormenting his central character. It is one more of his self-condemnations which are attempts at expiation.

* *Mark Twain and Southwestern Humor.*

The other of the two main forms that this nightmare of Mark Twain's takes is that of the Terrible Voyage. *Which Was It?*, though none of it may be meant to be actual, is close to the realism of *Pudd'nhead Wilson*, but the tale of the voyage is sheer fantasy. The best and longest of the manuscripts which are based on this theme, evidently written in the autumn of 1898, is that which, from a phrase in the notes for the story, has been known as *The Great Dark*. This begins, as others of these fragments do, with an affectionate domestic life and a children's birthday party. One of the little girl's birthday presents has been a microscope from her father, and the father, who is named Henry Edwards, is showing her how to work it. They examine a drop of stale water from a puddle and watch the behavior of the organisms which are seen to be living in it. Then, tired of romping with the children, the father throws himself on a sofa, falls asleep, and dreams that the drop of water is an ocean. He has a desire to explore these unknown waters, and he persuades the Superintendent of Dreams to provide him with a ship and a crew. His family are to go along. They start off in blustering and misty weather, and the mate confesses to Henry that not only does he not know where they are but that the captain doesn't know either. Disturbing monsters appear: one like a whale with hairy spidery legs and another "shaped like a woodlouse and as big as a turreted monitor, . . . racing by and tearing up the foam, in chase of a fat animal the size of an elephant and creased like a caterpillar." A man in a slouch hat and cloak appears and disappears. He is the Superintendent of Dreams with whom Henry has arranged the voyage. Henry becomes annoyed with this stranger because he finds he cannot make him give any explanation of what they are headed for. "If my style doesn't suit you," says the Superintendent, "you can end the dream as soon as

you please—right now, if you like." "He looked me steadily in the eye for a moment, then said, with deliberation
—'The dream? *Are you quite sure it is a dream?*' It took
my breath away. 'What do you mean? Isn't it a dream?'
He looked at me in that same way again; and it made my
blood chilly this time. Then he said—'You have spent
your whole life in this ship. And this is *real* life. Your
other life was the dream!' It was as if he had hit me, it
stunned me so. Still looking at me, his lip curled itself
into a mocking smile, and he wasted away like a mist and
disappeared. I sat a long time thinking uncomfortable
thoughts." Henry talks with his wife about the curious
weather. "I don't remember any different weather," she
says. It turns out that she cannot remember ever having
taken a voyage before—though they had made a trip to
Europe when their daughter Jessie was a year old. She
tells him that he must have dreamed this. Doesn't she remember that they crossed on the *Batavia* (as the Clemenses had actually done), doesn't she remember Captain
Moreland (its real captain)? Then she does begin to remember this trip, but still thinks it was only a dream. But
when he makes a reference to their home in Springport,
she cannot remember that. She remembers three other
"dream-homes," but when she talks to him about their life
there, he can recognize only an average of two out of
seven of the incidents she mentions. He finds that he
cannot, on his side, remember what she tells him of the
captain's young son having been eaten by a spider-squid.
On the ship, she gives birth to a boy. They continue to
discuss the past and to try to find details that they both
remember. Twelve years later—the voyage seems endless
—the same gigantic squid appears, grips the mast with its
long tentacles, and is trying to pull over the ship. "The
stench of his breath was suffocating everybody." (The
democratic masses that Mark Twain came to fear and

distrust?) They fire two thousand bullets at the creature's moonlike eyes, but blinded, it is not discouraged and continues to follow the ship. The children have disappeared, and Alice is in a panic, but they are found to have hidden in the hold. After this, the passengers divert themselves with concerts and private theatricals; but they do not know where they are or where they are sailing to, and after years of this, the crew mutinies. (The Homestead Strike of 1892 and other industrial disturbances?) The captain makes them a speech: "I don't know where this ship is, but she's in the hands of God, and that's enough for me, it's enough for you. . . . If it is God's will that we pull through, we pull through—otherwise not. We haven't had an observation for four months, but we are going ahead, and do our best to fetch up somewhere."

Here the main manuscript breaks off, but Mark Twain left notes as to what was to follow. These are mentioned by Mr. Lynn and summed up by Mr. De Voto, who gives only a facsimile of one of the pages in his edition of *Letters from the Earth,* but Mr. Tuckey merely refers us to this summary of Mr. De Voto's. It is annoying that, with all the pretensions of this MLA edition of the Mark Twain papers, such an important manuscript as *The Great Dark* should be given such skimpy treatment. Why are the notes not printed here along with the rest? It is difficult to tell from these summaries of them what, even in its tentative form, Mark Twain had imagined for the further adventures of this sinister and tragic voyage. It would seem that the captain quells the mutiny by agreeing to turn back; but the crew falsify the compass and steer by another in Henry's cabin, and the Superintendent of Dreams falsifies this one, too, as the result of which the crew cease to trust their leader (this is far from clear in De Voto's account). The ship is now becalmed; another ship, *The Two Darlings,* drifts near it (I have seen no proposed explanation of this second vessel's strange name).* There is supposed to be treasure on the ship, which the leader of the mutiny wants to steal, but this ship disappears in a snowstorm, and both the Edwardses' small son and the captain's daughter are for some reason carried away with it. The ship is pursued for ten years till the passengers' hair is turning gray. Suddenly they find themselves exposed to the glare of a "disastrous bright light"—from the reflector under the microscope slide— which entirely dries up the sea. *The Two Darlings* has been stranded there, too, but when they go to it, they discover that everyone on board has perished of hunger and thirst; they have been turned into mummified corpses.

The story was to end in a holocaust of horror. The captain goes mad from grief, the mutineer finds the treasure, but has also gone mad from thirst and "sits playing with it and blaspheming." The crew have had a drunken brawl, in which some of them have been killed. The Edwardses' daughter Jessie has been killed by a stray shot. Henry Edwards begs Alice not to look at the body of the little boy, but she does so and her grief is terrible. Two days later, everyone is dead except Henry and his Negro servant. "It is midnight," Mark Twain writes at the end of his notes. "Alice and the children come to say goodnight. I think them dreams. Think I am back in *a dream*."

In a letter to Howells of August 16, 1895, he says that he has dropped a "story to be called *Which Was the Dream?*" because he had come to see "that the plan was a totally impossible one—for me; but a new plan suggested itself . . . I think I've struck the right one this time . . . I feel that all of the first half of the story—and I hope three-fourths—will be comedy; but by the former plan the whole of it (except the first three chapters) would have

* A correspondent, Mr. George B. Alexander, suggests that *The Two Darlings* may apply to the girl and boy who are carried off by the ship.

been tragedy and unendurable, almost. I think I can carry
the reader a long way before he suspects that I am laying
a tragedy-trap." But how much would the ordinary readers of the nineties, the readers upon whom Mark Twain
depended, have enjoyed being caught in a tragedy-trap? I
believe that Mark Twain's inability to carry through any
of these narratives, on which he recurrently worked, was,
first, that they were so much out of key with the prev-
alent taste of the time that they could not have been
well received, for although there are traces in *The Great
Dark* of Mark Twain's characteristic humor, the narrative
as we have it exerts from beginning to end a malign and
powerful spell. A second consideration must have been
that he did not want to worry his wife by either tragic or
comic accounts of the conflicts in their married life. Yet
in the letter to Howells quoted above, he says that "Mrs.
Clemens is pretty outspokenly satisfied with" the story,
and she herself writes to a friend, "I have not known Mr.
Clemens for years to write with so much pleasure and
energy as he has done during this last summer." She had,
then, approved the story, but had she read it or merely
been told about it?

The MLA has been boasting so much of the diligence
of its editing and proofreading that I am gratified to be
able to note that on page 168 of *Which Was the Dream?*
Mr. Tuckey has apparently failed to notice that in the
sentence which commences twelve lines from the bottom,
the author has interchanged "the sham David" with "the
real David"; that on page 202 "romatic" has been printed
for "romantic," and that on page 339 "You're vain of it"
has been printed "You've vain of it."

As long as I am writing here about this recent work
which has been done on Mark Twain, I might mention
the serious shortcomings of Justin Kaplan's *Mr. Clemens
and Mark Twain.* This biography was received with en-

thusiasm and awarded a Pulitzer Prize and a National
Book Award. Mr. Kaplan has had at his disposal a good
deal of new material, and he has known how to present it
effectively. The book is very well worth reading if you are
interested in Mark Twain. But it brings to us no real revelation. The conception of Mark Twain as a divided personality, upon which the whole book is based, is by no
means a novel one. It was first introduced by Van Wyck
Brooks as long ago as 1920, but there is not a word of
acknowledgment to or even any mention of Brooks in *Mr.
Clemens and Mark Twain.* Nor can I find any mention
of the late Dixon Wecter, except as the editor of certain
Mark Twain letters, where an acknowledgment of quotations was inescapable. Now, Dixon Wecter had been
appointed executor of the Mark Twain papers and was the
author of *Sam Clemens of Hannibal,* the first volume of
a projected biography which Wecter did not live to complete. He was able to bring Mark Twain only up to 1853.
Mr. Kaplan's biography begins in 1867, when Mark
Twain came East from the West. He is at pains, in an
implausible preface, to justify what he calls "this abrupt-
ness" in taking up his subject at the age of thirty-one:
"He was always his own biographer," he says of Mark
Twain, "and the books he wrote about [his earlier] years
are incomparably the best possible accounts. . . . But the
central drama of his mature literary life was his discovery
of the usable past" (the phrase is another borrowing from
Brooks made to figure here in a stupid way). The conclusion seems unavoidable that Mr. Kaplan does not care to
give Wecter credit for having covered the early ground.
Nor does he mention *Mark Twain in Nevada,* by Effie
Mona Mack, which deals with the Western period.

   Mr. Kaplan thus rather indecently ignores three of his
important predecessors, and he betrays certain disqualifica-
tions for writing about Mark Twain at all. He seems not
really to appreciate Mark Twain as a writer and makes

almost no attempt to criticize his work. In writing about a
humorist, he shows little comprehension of humor. Of all
that made Mark Twain attractive to his public and his
own life, however guilt-ridden, enjoyable to himself, Mr.
Kaplan can give us little idea. For that we are obliged to
go to Albert Bigelow Paine's old biography, written in the
spirit of the period, in which we get all the bright and
expensive surface of trips to Europe on Cunarders, big
places in suburban Connecticut, good cigars with rich
businessmen, after-dinner speeches to crashes of laughter,
anniversary luncheons at Delmonico's. Mr. Kaplan's defects, to be sure, cannot be blamed on the MLA, but they
represent another department of the American Literature
industry: the competent journalistic hack as well as the
mediocre professor can make a reputation for himself by
seizing on some well-known author who has not yet been
made the subject of a biography and procuring a first
access to his papers. The biographer may not have the
least sympathy with the personality of the author or any
real interest in his work—as Mark Schorer does not seem
to have had in writing about Sinclair Lewis; but he is
prepared to spend years on his subject and knows that he
will be rewarded by acknowledgment of having been the
first to do a solid biography of this subject. It is true that,
in the case of Mark Twain, the work on him has until
lately been hampered and complicated by the insistence
of his surviving daughter on an almost Victorian censorship as well as by the mortality of his appointed executors,
which has proved to be as high as that of the Loeb trans-
lators of Josephus. Neither Bernard De Voto nor Wecter
lived long enough to finish what he had undertaken. In
this case, there could be no definitive biography as there
has been no definitive edition.

That the emergence of the United States as a self-
righteous but not self-confident "World Power" should

stimulate a boom in our literature and history—the importance of which was still in my college days of 1912–16 academically so much underestimated—and that this should, in the present period, have given rise to an exploitation which exaggerates its importance is not at all surprising. And the result of this has been that at the moment when we are playing our most odious role in the world and one most contradictory to our declared ideals, the study of both our literature and our history has taken on monstrous proportions as fields for academic activity. At Harvard there are now six professors occupied with American history to the two that teach modern European, and the bureaucrats of the MLA, abetted by their allies in Washington, are now, as I have shown above, directing a republication of our classics which is not only, for the most part, ill-judged and quite sterile in itself but even obstructive to their republication in any other form. It is, in general, to be sure, regrettable that the federal $1,700,-000 which had been authorized by the National Arts and Humanities Act should recently have been cut in half, in deference to the $80,000,000,000 demanded for what is called "Defense," but this does have one cheerful aspect: it is likely to cut down the boondoggling of the MLA editions.

In the meantime, there is no reason whatever that some unsubsidized publisher should not at least make a beginning of such a republication as I have proposed by bringing out in a cheaper and more complete as well as better-designed form an experimental edition of one of these writers. Contrary to arguments used by sponsors of the MLA, there are few difficulties of copyright, because almost all this material is now in the public domain. The publishers of the MLA Melville, I learn from the *Publishers Weekly* of July 29, 1968, have been debating the problems of protecting the copyright of the text of this

edition. But we should not need to use this text. We could
easily afford to ignore it. I do not know whether, from the
point of view of copyright, it would be feasible to take
over the English text of the Constable Standard Edition,
the only complete edition that has so far been published
anywhere. It was limited to 750 sets, but it has now, I
learn, been republished by Russell & Russell of New York
in a photographed reproduction, the sixteen volumes of
which sell for $135.

In order to show the feasibility as well as the desirability of bringing out the kind of editions I should like to
see, I shall suggest a few specific examples. There was no
satisfactory edition of Poe till 1902, when James A. Harrison of the University of Virginia brought out his
Virginia Edition (republished in large paper as the Mon-
ticello Edition). All the texts of Poe before that time
—including that of Stedman and Woodberry, which was
given a standing it did not deserve—had been based, so
far as I know, on that of the wretched Rufus Griswold,
who, as a detractor of Poe and a falsifier of his letters,
deserved the worst that Baudelaire said of him. Poe, at the
time of his death, was preparing a volume of his critical
writings, and this material Griswold patched together according to his own notions. James Harrison discovered
that the various printings of Poe's stories and poems "con-
flicted in so many points that no course was left except to
reject them all—beginning with Griswold, whom all had
more or less faithfully followed—and extract a new and
absolutely authentic text from the magazines, periodicals,
and books of tales and poems which Poe himself had
edited or to which he had contributed. . . . The chronological order of the tales being established, each tale was
made the subject of a separate and prolonged study in its
successive appearances in magazine, periodical or volume
form, the variants were carefully noted and that form of

the text was selected which had, directly or indirectly, the sanction of Poe himself."

In an unpretentious way, all these variants have been recorded in fine print at the end of each volume. James Harrison has thus done for Poe all that the MLA editors have boasted of doing for their authors, but, unlike them, has done nothing superfluous. Poe's critical articles have been straightened out and presented in the order in which they were first published, and there have been added a number of short book notices which Harrison attributes to Poe. This edition otherwise contains a good deal of uncollected and unpublished material, including what Harrison believed was the complete file of Poe's *Marginalia,* a series of reflections and opinions which seems to me a good deal more interesting than Baudelaire's imitation of it in *Mon Coeur Mis à Nu.* This edition also includes the first published collection of Poe's letters—superseded now, however, by that of John Ward Ostrom. To Harrison's compilation should be added such writings of Poe as have turned up since Harrison's edition: Poe's letters on *Doings of Gotham,* written for the *Columbia Spy,* the files of which were only recovered in 1928; the articles on cryptography in *Alexander's Weekly Messenger,* in which it appears that, as Poe had boasted elsewhere and as some had not been ready to believe, he had actually succeeded in solving all the cryptograms that had been sent him each month by his readers; as well as, I understand, some further installments of the *Marginalia.* Harrison's edition, if possible, should be checked with the materials of the late Thomas Mabbott, who believed he had grounds for discrediting some of Harrison's attributions of unsigned articles to Poe—if the publication of Mabbott's edition should, indeed, not be preferred to Harrison's—and the whole subject should otherwise be brought up to date.

As for other possibilities: the whole of Stephen Crane, I should think, could be collected in one not too fat volume. If the whole of Balzac—that is, of *La Comédie Humaine*—can be got into ten volumes in the Pléiade, it should be possible to get the whole of Henry James into as few or perhaps less. The editor best qualified for this, Mr. Leon Edel, would already have done most of the required work. I suggest that it is really not necessary to note all the variants of the texts of Henry James from their first periodical appearances to the much revised New York Edition. A few specimens of these last revisions—such as Ford Madox Ford provides in his book on Henry James—would, I should think, except perhaps for a full account of the changes in *The Turn of the Screw*, be quite enough for the purposes of the ordinary reader.

The editors of such a series rather than of volumes in the MLA editions would seem to the non-academic writer to have little or nothing to lose. They would be signing contracts directly with a publisher, and those contracts would provide for both advances and royalties. A professional writer is astounded by the terms accepted by academic persons for work that may take many years. It seems incredible that, in the case of university presses, they sometimes have no contracts at all, receive no royalties at all, and have never had a penny for their trouble. They think in terms of academic prestige, and it is time that some solid achievement in this line should be given some more solid compensation. To examine an MLA contract gives a professional writer the shudders. The Board of Editors "agrees to make available to the Editor to the best of its power and judgment funds emanating from the CEAA [Center for Editions of American Authors] in support of the —— Edition; and to cooperate to the best of its ability in supporting any attempt by the Editor to secure grants in aid of his work for the —— Edition from his

University, from foundations, or from any other source."
The first of these promises means that the editor's needs
will be met for travel or other expenses involved in the
checking of books or manuscripts; the second, that he will
have to rustle for himself for any further payment but that
the Center will recommend him. The final clause of the
agreement stipulates that "no person will receive royalties
of any sort from the sale of any volume of the —— Edition. Should the —— Edition ever repay its publishing
costs to the Press, any further profits will be divided between CEAA and the —— University Foundation." The
editor, then, is not promised a dollar beyond his expense
account, but it seems that this expense account—supple-
mented by a grant?—may be stretched to a year or more
off from his regular teaching job. This encourages the
boondoggling mentioned above in connection with the
Mark Twain industry—that is, prolonged payment for
boring work and a waste of the time which would be
better devoted to bringing out our unfortunate classics.


This article in a slightly different form first appeared in
the issues of *The New York Review of Books* of September 26 and October 10, 1968. It provoked a good deal of
correspondence, some of it letters to the paper and some
of it letters to me personally. A selection from the former
was published in the *Review* of December 19. Among
both classes of letters were many from academic persons
and publishers supporting my point of view. On the other
hand, we received from the colleges epistles of a violence
and venom that rather surprised us, though I suppose we
ought to have expected it.

Mr. Ronald Gottesman of Indiana University, the
"Textual Editor" for *Their Wedding Journey,* announces
in his first paragraph that he will limit himself "to clarify-

ing one of his [my] basic confusions, correcting a few of his blatant errors, rereading some of his more grotesque distortions, and answering a couple of his charming questions." My heinous "factual errors," he goes on to explain, are as follows: I referred to the Indiana University Press as the University of Indiana Press. But I made a point of not so referring to it, having learned from a previous experience that this university is outraged if it is not called Indiana University. But why can it not be referred to in the same way as any other state university? However, I had deferred to its wish. It was the editors of *The New York Review* who listed the book I was dealing with as published by the University of Indiana. My next errors —corrected above—are that Reedy Professor of English had got printed as Rudy Professor of English, and that Mr. Reeves had "had the support of two Associate not Assistant Textual Editors (as the title page states plainly)." What is the difference between an Associate and an Assistant Editor? Some academic distinction? It can hardly, I suppose, be denied that these editors assisted Mr. Reeves. I have here removed any possible cause for complaint by writing "assistant" lower case. Next, in speaking of the Centenary Edition of the MLA's *Marble Faun,* I said that it had 610 pages, then stated that it contained 467 pages of Hawthorne and 232 of textual apparatus. I have made a recount of these latter pages and now make them 259; Mr. Gottesman seems to have failed to notice that the 610 pages of the main body of the book are preceded by 138 preliminary pages numbered with Roman numerals. "Mr. Wilson must also be called to account for distortions." Only one distortion is mentioned: that I wrote in such a way as to make it seem that the Marches' comparison of the modern American aqueducts with the Roman ones occurred on their first wedding journey instead of on a trip made twelve years later. Was it really worthwhile to note this: the state of mind of the Marches in regard to the United States and Europe was still more or less the same. Mr. Gottesman here gives up the idea of exposing several "grotesque distortions": "I am trying to be brief and factual and so will let the matter rest with this one vivid example of Mr. Wilson's carelessness and irresponsibility." He ends by remarking, "Just for the record, *Their Wedding Journey* is . . . an exceptionally handsome piece of bookmaking." I did not deny this: I said that it was impracticable.

Mr. Paul Baender, who is the Secretary of the Iowa–California Edition of Mark Twain (and who misuses the word *demean* as many people of course do, but as a college professor should not), writes that his edition and the MLA edition of the Mark Twain papers are two different projects, which I did not deny. He says that my description, derived from an earlier correspondent, "of the collation program here at Iowa is misleading and wrong. The most reliable way of discovering variations among different typesettings of a work is to assemble a group of proofreaders and have one of them read aloud from a certain typesetting while the rest are following in the others. The point is to determine from variants that turn up whether the author made changes from edition to edition. One necessary precaution is to keep the silent proofreaders from reading ahead of the book that is read aloud, and the most common means of control is to have the speaker read very slowly and without intonation. The man in charge of this operation for *Huckleberry Finn*—not *Tom Sawyer*—thought at first that he might get a surer control by having the text read backward. *But the method was abandoned because it was too irritating and because it did not seem more reliable than the other method.* Reading backward has never been part of our standard procedure, and if other editors in the project have tried it, they have done so on their own. The Hinman Collating Machine did *not* show that there are no 'serious problems about either the text [of *Tom Sawyer*] or the alterations Mark Twain made in it.' The Hinman machine can only compare specimens from a single typesetting, and so its results in any case can have no bearing upon other settings or upon the relations between manuscripts and printings. As a matter of fact, the text of *Tom Sawyer* presents unusually serious problems. Two manuscripts survive, Mark Twain's original and a secretarial copy that contains scribal errors and author's revisions. The first American edition was set from the original, the first English from the secretarial copy. The need for close checking and elaborate tabulations should be obvious." He adds that there should be no allowances made for my "display of ignorance, unreason, infantilism and meanness." Apropos of my proposal for an American Pléiade series, he remarks, "If I were to read *Maggie* in his proposed one-volume Crane, it would weigh as much as the entire volume—say five or six pounds—and surely that is too much." Mr. Baender can never have seen the Pléiade editions. The largest volume of the Pléiade I happen to have, which contains the complete works of Montaigne and runs to 1,791 pages, weighs exactly two pounds.

Mr. Richard M. Fletcher of the English Department of Edinboro State College, Pennsylvania, speaks of my "facetious name-dropping and air of petulant ill-humor." The name-dropping, it seems, consists of my having, in the letter describing my project, addressed my old friend Jason Epstein as "Jason"—"Isn't it nice," says Mr. Fletcher, "that Edmund knows people in the publishing business so intimately?"—and of having mentioned that André Malraux had sent me some information about French government subsidies to literature. Most of the rest of the letter makes no sense at all, but there seems to be an implication that since I am a graduate of Princeton and since the issue of *The New York Review* in which my first installment appeared carried also an advertisement of the Princeton University Press, my articles were a part of a Princeton conspiracy.

On the other side, *The New York Review* and I have, as I say, received many sympathetic letters.

Mr. William H. Y. Hackett, Jr., director of the Bobbs-Merrill Company, expresses a publisher's point of view:

While the desire of the MLA to "purify" the texts of American literature is both legitimate and worthy, they have used their standing as scholars and their positions in the university establishment to create a monopoly on what is in reality a national resource, in the public domain. They hold that passing a public domain text such as *The Scarlet Letter* through the Hinman Collating Machine gives them copyright protection; they choose to forget their action restricts the free use of a national treasure that is our common property.

The federal government, recognizing the value of authoritative texts of Hawthorne, Melville, Howells, Twain, and other great American authors has appropriated funds to help accomplish this program. With the acquisition of such funds some scholars by changing hats and becoming administrators have lost perspective in the heady atmosphere of money, influence, and power. Perhaps, defensively or in unconscious awareness that most academics turned administrator will trade an ounce of power for a pound of principle, they have joined forces and retreated to their own medieval castle of academic respectability. The moat is MLA, PMLA, and CEAA; the wall, coöperating university presses (supported by tax exemptions); the portcullis, scholarship; and the keep, the CEAA imprimatur and copyright. (Is the Hinman Collating Machine alive? Does it breathe? Is it an author? How about Hawthorne's thumb smudges?)

Of what are these self-appointed authorities afraid? (Daley's yippies?) If they are so desirous of providing authentic texts to American and world readers, why don't they release their work at a low price and right now? In fairness, we should receive what we, as taxpayers, are paying for. It's unbelievable that Howells' *Their Wedding Journey* costs the reading public $10.00 a copy when the following formula is considered: A professor, paid by state funds (X), performs research financed by federal funds (Y), that is published by a public press (Z)— $X + Y + Z = \$10.00$ cost to the public.

My attention has been called to a kind of controversy which has been going on in regard to the MLA edition of *The House of the Seven Gables*. It appears that, in 1964, before the Ohio volume came out in 1965, Mr. Hyatt H. Waggoner of Brown University had published in the Riverside Editions series a carefully collated text of this novel. Mr. Bowers had stated at the end of his textual introduction to the Centenary volume that the text of the book was "established here for the first time in the relative purity of its manuscript form"; but he was obliged to add a footnote explaining that Mr. Waggoner's edition had reached him only when "this Introduction was in proof," so that his statement was "no longer true. However, the Riverside text will be found to differ considerably from the Centenary text in its manuscript and its estimate of the amount of authorial proof-correction." Mr. Waggoner had made his collation between the manuscript and the first edition without the Hinman machine or the help of teams of graduate students, and he had discovered that a comma inserted by Hawthorne after the word "solitude" in the first sentence of the last paragraph of the book—

"Maule's Well, all this time, though left in solitude," etc.
—did not exist in certain copies of the first edition. This
seems somewhat to have upset the workers on the Ohio
Centenary Edition, and one of them expressed disbelief
that Mr. Waggoner could have found this out himself
without having used a machine or come upon some reference to this omission in the Houghton Mifflin files. Mr.
Bowers, without acknowledgment, was obliged to note this
discrepancy in his textual introduction. Mr. Waggoner
had also accepted, as Mr. Bowers had not done, the
printer's emendation of "barn-yard fowl" from the "barn-
door fowl" of the manuscript. Mr. Bowers consulted the
big Oxford Dictionary and found references to "barn-door
fowl" in authors as late as Scott and decided, no doubt
correctly, to let Hawthorne's phrasing stand. This does
have a very slight interest in showing Hawthorne's old-
fashioned usage, and in comparison with the editors' other
findings, it comes to seem almost sensational.

This affair of the editions of *The House of the Seven
Gables* is discussed at some length in a contribution by
Mr. Richard Harter Fogle of the University of North
Carolina to the 1965 volume of the annual called *American Literary Scholarship*. In comparing the Waggoner
edition with that of the Centenary Edition, Mr. Fogle
comes to the conclusion that the two texts of the book
"are both admirable in themselves. The Riverside Edition
is greatly preferable in critical acumen and general humanity. Despite the enormous competence and industry
behind the Centenary volume . . . , its pleasures are intended for highly specialized bibliographers, and steadfast
literary historians of a type that are now rather to be
respected than heeded. When this definitive edition of
Hawthorne was announced I was prepared, with what
now seems undue innocence, to welcome it wholeheart-
edly. It quickly appeared, however, that its concern with

Hawthorne as an important and unique American writer
was small; he was merely a corpus of important texts upon
which scholars could exercise their virtuosity. Mr. Bowers
has used his undoubted talents largely in praise of his own
vocation of bibliography, and Mr. Charvat [one of the
three "General Editors" of the Centenary Edition] has
employed his great knowledge of literary history and of
bookmaking chiefly in reassuring us that Hawthorne is
now safely accounted for as a normal nineteenth-century
American with a turn for literature, and may consequently
be filed and forgotten."

One of the letters that have interested me most is from
Mr. T. D. Besterman, the internationally known scholar
who is the director of the Institut et Musée Voltaire at
Geneva:

Mr. Wilson's article shines with good intentions, but he
has got some of his facts wrong and his basic assumption
is false. I am also sad that he has swallowed whole
M. Malraux's propaganda pill. Sancta simplicitas! How
can Mr. Wilson have overlooked the strings attached to
the French government's literary subsidies?
One of the mistakes Mr. Wilson has made is to repro-
duce M. Malraux's claims without checking them. For
instance, I am mildly surprised to learn that among the
projects he is patronising is a critical edition of the complete correspondence of Voltaire. This edition was in fact
published by the Voltaire Institute of Geneva in 1953–
1965, without help or subsidy of any kind from any
French organism. A new edition is now in the press as
part of Voltaire's complete works, again undertaken without subsidy of any kind.
And this brings me to the essential defect of Mr. Wilson's reasoning. He has swallowed hook, line and sinker

the notion that no major editorial job can be undertaken without the help of a "factory." Pray forgive me for mentioning that my edition of Voltaire's correspondence was a fairly substantial undertaking—20,000 letters, hundreds of appendixes, tens of thousands of notes, 107 volumes. Yet it was planned and carried out single-handed, with one secretary and, for part of the time, one assistant. Why then all this fuss about councils and foundations? A World's Classics or Pléiade type of edition would be a sound commercial venture, well within the capacity of any major publisher, if only the "factory" syndrome could be cured.

Theodore Besterman

I do not understand why Mr. Besterman should suppose that I believe in the "factory" system of editing. This was one of the assumptions I was trying to discredit.

December 1968

# THE MONSTERS OF BOMARZO

Among the uniform amenities of Italy there is one patch of ugliness and horror. The Orsini Park of Bomarzo strikes a deliberately discordant note. The explanation of this strange phenomenon has so far been hidden in mystery, and the best one can do about describing it is to begin by recounting its legend. According to this somewhat fantastic story, one of the Orsini dukes, whose real name was Pier Francesco but who was known by the nickname Vicino, designed toward the end of the sixteenth century a garden of a sensationally eccentric kind, which exhibited a varied assortment of grotesque and horripilating figures, executed in the soft local tufa by a captive from the battle of Lepanto.

The duke was a hunchback and is said to have been embittered by an affair of his wife with a younger brother. The duke had this brother murdered and had his own life memorialized by a collection of monstrosities created as a gesture of defiant misanthropy. A sign dedicates the gardens "to the somber character of Pier Francesco Orsini, who, retiring on his estate, in 1560, had the labors begun which expressed his anguish. . . . Vicino was a hunch-

back and deformed. . . . His attractive wife, Giulia Far-
nese, and a very handsome brother [fell in love]. He killed
the brother, knowing that Giulia loved her kinsman."

A compiler of a work called *Famous Men* describes
Vicino as of "regal appearance and way of life, a lover of
arms and letters," and speaks of him as still alive toward
1574. A letter to him of 1564 refers to the "marvels of
Bomarzo" and advises him how to represent in his castle
"the story of the giants." It says that the idea is "in har-
mony with the place, where there are so many other
extravagant and supernatural things." These references
seem to be all that is actually recorded of Bomarzo. Mario
Praz has written about it—though more briefly than one
might expect on the part of that amateur of curiosities—in
his *Panopticon Romano* and even more briefly in another
of his books, *Bellezza e Bizzarria*.

The only book, so far as I know, exclusively devoted to
the subject is *Les Monstres de Bomarzo* by a Frenchman,
André Pieyre de Mandiargues, who has done some research among the family papers in the archives of the
Capitol in Rome, though he has not been able to consult
certain documents in the possession of the present Orsini
princes or some other possible sources of information; and
he has finally come to the conclusion that, for reasons he
does not know—it may be that the monsters were a scandal—the real story has been suppressed. "One is baffled by
so tenacious an obscurity," M. de Mandiargues says.
"From the moment one undertakes to dig a little into
questions that are posed by the monuments of Bomarzo,
the darkness that lies at their feet is so thick that it would
seem that it has been accumulated intentionally." What is
striking is not only that the Italians do not investigate
Bomarzo but that they do not seem to want to know about
it. An attempt has been made to get Mondadori to have
de Mandiargues's book translated, but this has been unsuccessful.

The Italians like to have their art pleasing—harmonious, well-proportioned. Even the roughness and horror of Dante's Hell are later counteracted by his Purgatory and Paradise. It has been said that the monsters of Bomarzo are a kind of thing that would seem more appropriate in Germany, with its taste for the macabre and grotesque. They were, at any rate, for four centuries left to themselves, embedded in a jungle of shrubbery. My old Baedeker of 1909 does not mention Bomarzo at all, but a *Guida ai Misteri e Segreti del Lazio* gives it five pages and four photographs. When de Mandiargues visited Bomarzo— his book is dated 1957—he says that the jungle was undisturbed, but that he was sure that it was only a question of time before it would be barred off by a barbed-wire fence and tickets would be sold at a wicket. When I went there in 1968, a fence and the wicket were already in existence, and the jungle had been partly cleared, though not enough to make it easy going.

The difficulty of getting far enough from the statues on account of the bushes and trees which surround them makes it impossible to take good photographs—even those of de Mandiargues's book are rather unsatisfactory. The old steps that lead down the hill are so worn down that descent is difficult. Apparently only foreigners till very recently have come to Bomarzo. Signore Praz, though he has lived in Rome the greater part of his life and though Bomarzo is not far beyond Orvieto, says that he had never heard of it till he was told about it by a Russian painter, who had himself learned about it from an American. When Praz inquired of a local guide whether many people came to see it, he was told "with a disconsolate nod," "Americans and Canadians every day." The park was, at last, however, disclosed with characteristic showmanship by the Spanish Salvador Dali, a friend of the Russian painter who had told Mario Praz about it. Dali, as it were, "took possession," as Mario Praz puts it, with a procession of motorcars and a retinue that suggested the making of a film.

Bomarzo is of course a wonderful find for surrealists like Dali. A product of Renaissance extravagance, it falls in all too appropriately with their cult of the irrational and the nightmarish. It seems to me that de Mandiargues's book is perhaps a little warped by his surrealist glee at finding that such effects were already being achieved at the end of the sixteenth century. Mario Praz has pointed out that, from a period earlier by a century, there stands at the entrance to the gardens of the Palazzo Zuccari in Rome something similar to the Bomarzo ogre, a great gaping mask with eyes for windows, through the mouth of which one enters. This was designed by Federigo Zuccaro, and Praz calls attention to the fact that the letter from Federigo which advises Orsini on his project for representing the "story of the giants" recommends for this purpose his brother Taddeo, a "mannerist," which implies an aptitude for distorted images.

The imposing Palazzo Orsini stands at the top of a very steep hill, from which it overhangs and dominates the flock of monsters browsing below. I was sorry I could not visit it because I had only a day at Bomarzo, and this palazzo for some reason seems inaccessible from the inn at which we dined. A few of the rooms have been taken over by the Commune (the town hall), in which the mayor has his offices, but the immense unused chambers of the building contain at least one sinister mystery: a mummified human body, with closed slits of eyes, a hole for a nose, and a mouthful of long grisly teeth, who is crowned with a wreath of flowers and richly dressed in a beribboned costume, now falling to tarnished decay. The mummy is protected by a lid of glass. M. de Mandiargues, though he includes a photograph of it, throws no light on this gruesome figure except to note that it is "evidently not so old as the statues."

From the palazzo down the hill the show begins. Near the top, one is soon confronted by the gaping jaws of an ogre, through which one passes into a room furnished with a stone bench that rather recalls a Mithraic chapel. On the upper lip of this ogre is a curved and uncanny inscription, *"Ogni pensiero vol [a?]"* ("Every thought flies"), the last word of which is now defaced. What exactly does this imply? One would like to see these inscriptions collected and studied for their authorship and meaning. Some are intended to astonish, perhaps terrify the visitor: *"Voi che pel mondo gite errando vaghi de veder meraviglie alte et stupende venite qua dove son faccie horrende elephanti leoni orse orche et draghi"* ("You who go wandering about the world, in the desire to see high and astounding wonders: come here where there are horrid faces, elephants, lions, bears, ogres, and dragons"); *"Notte et giorno noi siam vigili e pronte a guardar dogni injuria questa fonte"* ("Night and day we are on the watch and ready to defend this fountain from any damage"); and on one of the monstrous stone urns: *"Fonte non fu tra chi [h]a guardia sia delle piu strane belve"* ("Fountain never was which had stranger beasts as a guard"); below one of the crouching sphinxes:

> *Che con ciglia inarcati et labbra strette*
> *non va per questo loco, manco ammira*
> *le famose del mondo moli sette.*

("He who with lifted eyebrows and lips compressed does not go through this place does not even admire the seven wonders of the world"); *"Dimmi poi se tante meraviglie sien fatte per inganno or per arte"* ("Tell me then whether such marvels are produced by trickery or by art").

Farther along past the gaping ogre, a more than life-size elephant with a kind of castle on its back and a male figure, with a kind of drum on his head, squatting on the elephant's forehead, is mauling a man with its trunk and probably about to kill him. In a shallow and stagnant pool sits a river god with Neptune-like beard and drenched hair, who, unlike the usual statues in fountains, has a disagreeable snub nose and an unfriendly expression of a kind which is typical of the whole garden. A ferocious winged dragon is keeping two lions at bay. Two figures, perhaps twenty feet tall, are engaged in a terrible combat. One holds the other upside down and is apparently rending his legs asunder, while the other with open mouth is howling. There is a theory that this group is intended for Hercules destroying Cacus, the cattle thief, but I could detect no distinguishing traits that made such an identification plausible. One could not even be sure of the sex of the victim, who by some is thought to be a woman.

I had to wait by this group for some time, guarding my companion's handbag, while she went to the bottom of the hill to report on what was to be found below. I saw that the towering statues had now been anchored to the rock behind them to prevent them from toppling over. They were accompanied by an object like a huge phallus, which seemed to have been cut from the same rock formation, toward which a badly eroded but somewhat ducklike creature was apparently opening its beak. A rhyming inscription as follows: *"Se rodi altier gia fu de suo colosso pur di quest il mio bosco anche si gloria e per piu non poter fo quant io posso"* ("If Rhodes was once proud of its colossus, my wood can also boast of this one and I can do no more than I am able"). Of another inscription, mostly effaced, one can only read the words *"—scempio sanglante"* ("bloody slaughter").

Creeping vines; lichens on the statues; little blue, white, and yellow flowers; some conifers and low saplings. A stagnant pool; a little cascade that is falling from beneath big elephant-ear-like leaves which have been eaten full of holes. Below, beyond the foot of the hill, one looks out on the familiar gray olive grove. There is a relatively chaste little temple said to be intended as a memorial to Orsini's first wife. On this or some other such building is the Latin admonition: *"Animus qui ascendo fit prudentior"* ("The spirit, by climbing here, is made more cautious"). But otherwise the ugly-grotesque is reiterated in many forms. A fishlike goggle-eyed face— wide nostrils and shaggy brows—stares out of a dried-up pool; it balances a sphere, surmounted by a castle. A whale stretches huge square-toothed jaws. The size of these creations is shown in one of de Mandiargues's photographs, in which a living young local girl, long-haired and bare-legged, is made to lie in relaxation below the maw of the whale, which dwarfs her at the same time that it emphasizes her attractiveness. An equally enormous tortoise is lurking among the trees at the side. On its shell stands a pedestal with another sphere and a female figure posing on the sphere.

Are these emblems of the Orsini family? The Orsini bears are in evidence, clasping to their bosoms large rosettes. There are sphinxes and women with urns on their heads, out of which grow weedy wild plants. Some of these female torsos seem to rear their heads with a certain nobility. But as we go farther, these partially disfigured shapes seem to convey erotic suggestion, and this has prompted a theory that the gardens were used as a stage for sexual orgies. A large moss-covered woman is lying on her back with her legs apart; a nymph has been evidently contrived to shoot a stream of water from between her legs; a monkey is embracing a woman from behind; two women in a strange ornamental row of figures of which one cannot make out the sense have

either a man or a woman—it is impossible to tell which—
upside down between them; a headless figure with female breasts and a thick scaled serpent's tail rears her
full-bosomed torso from the ground; a damaged hermaph-
rodite stands upright in a niche.

Broken fragments are half-buried in the earth below.
M. de Mandiargues says that the boys of the neighborhood have been shooting at the statues with slingshots
and that their disfigurement is partly due to this. At the
bottom of the hill, I was told, is some kind of larger
temple, which I did not go down to see.

There is a long novel, now translated, by an Argentine
writer, Manuel Mujica-Lainez, based on and entitled
*Bomarzo,* and this has provided Alberto Ginastera, the
Argentine composer, with his opera of the same name.
It is perhaps an evidence of the spell of Bomarzo that,
according to the album of the opera, Señor Mujica-
Lainez should believe he has identified himself with the
humpbacked duke. " 'I found that things I invented I
had not invented,' says the languid, mystical, brocade-
vested Argentine, waving a bejeweled hand. 'It was my
own life. The duke and I are one. . . .' " But the novel
and the opera largely follow the legend and do not dwell
much on the monsters. The duke is here represented as a
tragic neurotic case, bullied for his deformity by his
father and his brothers, and everything is shown through
a somber veil of self-hatred and apprehension. All the
resources of twelve-tone music for hideous and weird effects—which turn out to be very considerable—are exploited to the utmost here. There is a ballet of monsters
and a dance by the mummy.

The opera was forbidden by the mayor of Buenos Aires
on account of its alleged sexuality. But a scene between
Vicino and a Florentine courtesan, with whom he hopes
to lose his psychological impotence, must surely be the

least seductive scene of the kind that has ever been seen on the stage. The courtesan's boastful song about the talents of Florentine courtesans comes through as something soft and plaintive. This character, at the première in Washington, seemed to be wearing false naked breasts, and her chamber is lined with mirrors by which Vicino is cruelly halted when he sees his deformity multiplied. There is nothing but horror, with an undertone of pathos, from beginning to end of this opera, which I found nevertheless quite effective.

One feels in the park itself that the avoidance of it by the Italians is due to the same superstitious shrinking that makes them fear the evil eye and shy away from physical defects, and that the place does seem somehow accursed. It is a kind of malignant poem created by a determinedly perverse nature, which still speaks through its threatening inscriptions and petrified but animated dreams. It should certainly be cleared and preserved, and as far as possible reconstructed. It constitutes a kind of drama of the fantasy of the Renaissance, carried to violent and outrageous lengths. One wonders what had really happened to this supposedly anguished duke who has succeeded in realizing his sadistic and unpleasing vision. If he wanted to shock the Italians, his creation has not entirely lost its force. In any case, it deserves a study more searching than that of de Mandiargues.

1972

EDITOR'S NOTE: Edmund Wilson's article on the Bomarzo monsters would most certainly have been revised by him had he been able to complete the editing of this book. He had received a letter dated 10 February 1972 from Manuel Mujica-Lainez, author of a historical fiction about Bomarzo, saying that some of the "facts" in circulation about the statues had been derived from his own inventions in his novel. Wilson replied, "I was amused to know that the legend of the hunchback Orsini duke had been invented by you." He added he welcomed information on further sources and would try to look them up before reprinting the essay. Whether he found time to look them up we have no way of knowing. Elena Wilson believes Edmund would have liked to revisit Italy and see the statues again: he had first seen them during a stay in Rome in late April of 1967 when he was en route to Israel to bring his book on the Dead Sea scrolls up to date. But his health permitted no further travels. It has seemed advisable to let his essay stand here with whatever imperfections it may have, as evidence of Wilson's unflagging curiosity and the intensity with which he reached out to a subject that challenged his imagination.

# INDEX